Homework Made Simple

Tips, Tools, and Solutions
for Stress-Free Homework

Ann K. Dolin, M.Ed.

ADVANTAGE BOOKS
Washington, DC

5/29/2012

Homework Made
Simple

Tips, Tools, and Solutions
for Stress-Free Homework

Advantage Books

ISBN13: 978-0-9714609-8-0

ISBN10: 0-9714609-8-1

Published by Advantage Books, LLC
3268 Arcadia Pl NW
Washington, DC 20015
www.advantagebooks.net

Cover and graphics by Vatsana Design
Photographer: Wade Chi
Illustrator Page 27: Andrea Greenwich

The material in this book is based solely on the experience of the author
and is intended for informational purposes only. This book is not meant as
a substitute for medical or psychological advice or treatment and should not
be construed as such. Identifying information for all stories contained in
this book has been changed to protect the privacy of the individual and his
or her family.

Manufactured in the United States of America

10 9 8 7 6 5 4 3 2

Dedication

To my husband, Chris — without your encouragement and unconditional love, this book would not be possible. Thank you for holding down the fort while I worked long hours, nights, and weekends to finish this book. I could not have done it without you.

To my sons, Will and Ethan — the stars in my sky.

And finally, to all of my family, friends, and colleagues who have supported me through this endeavor — thank you.

Table of Contents

Part III   Troubleshooting: From Study Skills to Sticky Situations

Preface

What I Have Learned From Thousands of Families

Helping your child with homework can be a humbling experience. Nightly all across America, hundreds of thousands of parents ask their children the same question, "Is your homework done yet?" That question is so often answered with "Not yet, but I'll do it when I get to the next level of this video game," or even worse, "I told you, Mom, I don't have any tonight!"

All too often, we find ourselves cast in the role of the nightly homework police and the divide that this role creates between us and our kids can be one of the most painful aspects of parenting. My discovery of this dilemma came first as a teacher when my students' parents were honest enough to share with me what was really going on in their homes. Later on, as a tutor, problems with homework were the principal concern I heard parents express. And now, as a parent, I see the rest of the picture. It was through these three life experiences that my quest for practical, simple solutions to homework challenges began.

In 1998, I made the difficult decision to leave my public school classroom teaching position in Fairfax County, Virginia. I took a leap of faith and started my own business, Educational Connections Inc., a firm that provides tutoring to students in their homes on a one-to-one basis. In the beginning, I tutored on my own as my company's sole employee. Since then the company has grown to employ over 140 instructors throughout the metropolitan Washington, D.C. area and has successfully worked with over 4,000 students from kindergarten to college.

It became clear to me in the early years that many of my students lacked the foundational skills so often not taught in the classroom: organization, time management, and effective study methods. More and more, my tutors and I began incorporating these skills into our lessons in reading, writing, and math; and it worked. Our students' grades improved as they became more efficient learners. However, helping the kids solved only half the problem. Their parents also needed strategies at home in order to take the stress and frustration out of homework. When both child and parent were involved in the process not only did we see far greater progress, we saw much happier families as well.

This change takes place very differently in every home because each child has a unique set of skills and abilities. For that reason alone there is no one cure-all for homework challenges. The solutions that I use as a consultant and will share with you in this book are diverse and reflect the specific problems each student is encountering. Some kids procrastinate, some work too quickly without much effort, and some refuse to do homework altogether. My experiences with children of all ages have led me to define the six most common homework profiles that students often present when pressured by homework. They are:

The Disorganized

Almost all of my students struggled to stay organized. This problem is not uncommon, but it can challenge even the smartest kid and his parents. My disorganized students struggled in two main areas – materials and time. I found that if they had a cluttered backpack, they often had a poor sense of time management as well. These children fared much better when I taught them strategies and systems for staying organized. Furthermore, when their parents learned how to reinforce these newly designed systems, results improved.

The Rusher

Working too quickly or without attention to detail was a common challenge. Many of my students were very bright kids who processed information quickly. These perfectly capable children loved working at a rapid pace because they got their homework done faster. The problem was that their answers didn't necessarily reflect their abilities because they made careless errors. Other students rushed through work and slapped down subpar answers because they did not know how to deal with the assignment at hand. Both types of rushers required lots of positive reinforcement and needed to learn specific strategies to tackle their work habits.

The Procrastinator

Far and away, the homework challenge that parents complained about the most was procrastination. Not only did they have to poke and prod their children to start homework on a daily basis, but they also had to deal with the frustration presented by assignments that weren't due the next day – book reports, projects, and research papers. All of these tasks required long-term planning, an area in which their kids faltered. Although it would have been easy for me to swoop in, set up a plan of action, and finish the project with the child, I knew this wasn't the long-term solution. I saw myself as the intermediary who could teach the parents how to tackle these issues long after I left. Once I showed these parents step-by-step time management strategies, procrastination was brought under control.

The Avoider

Avoiders were, hands down, my toughest students to help. Some felt overwhelmed and underprepared (of course, they didn't want to admit it) and needed intense tutoring to dig themselves out of the hole that was already quite deep. Others had experienced so much disapproval and felt they had very little control of their lives. They lashed out by defiantly refusing to do something they could control – homework. Regardless of the reasons they evaded homework, my students considered total avoidance as their only way to cope. Fortunately, I found they could turn their academic careers around when the right approaches were used. For many students that involved allowing them to be a part of the decision-making process.

The Inattentive

Another common thread that my homework-challenged kids faced was a short attention span. Don't get me wrong – these kids could pay attention – there was no other way they could fixate on video games for hours on end. The problem was that they could not focus for extended periods of time on tasks they didn't find appealing. My students wanted to pay better attention. They just didn't know how and their parents comments like "pay attention" or "come on, focus" weren't making a difference. I had to employ novel strategies to help these kids, and each child's issues with attention were so very different.

Easily Frustrated

Tears, meltdowns, and yelling matches are common in households with kids that display a low threshold for frustration. When most students come across a math problem they don't know, they'll try a few times and ask for help if all else fails. But easily frustrated kids are usually reduced to tears at the first sign of an obstacle. If they aren't able to correctly answer a problem, they shut down instead of trying to work it out. As a tutor, I didn't always see this side of my students; they saved it all for the people they felt most comfortable around – their parents.

But when Mom and Dad tried to talk their kids out of the mood they were in, it rarely worked. Instead, I helped these families to strategize and to find ways out of the power struggles, meltdowns, and escalating frustrations.

Homework Made Simple Born

Helping families take the conflict out of homework in their homes has been one of my most rewarding experiences, but I didn't get into this line of work by design. About eight years ago, I was asked by a PTA mom to speak at her child's elementary school. The topic she requested? Homework, of course. She predicted the usual turnout of about 15 parents. So when I walked into the room to see over 100 parents in front of me, I was taken aback. From the look on her face, I knew she was shocked as well. As I set up the microphone and passed around the handouts, I could hear chatting in the background: "Homework is ruining our lives!", "He's up until 10:30 every night.", "I can't take these book reports anymore!" Their feelings of anxiety and pressure were palpable.

It was the topic of homework that brought these parents off the practice field, away from work, and out of the house, to attend that evening. After this experience, I knew I was on to something. Parents were desperate to learn how to take the stress out of homework. Even now, this topic is still the most requested. The tips, tools, and solutions I share with parents in my consulting work and through school presentations, I now share with you in this book, *Homework Made Simple*.

Part I

Getting Started

Katie slumped over the kitchen table with her head held tightly in her hands. After a stressful day at school and a long bus ride home, the last thing she wanted was more schoolwork. With tears flowing down her cheeks, she sobbed, "This is just so stupid. I don't care about dividing fractions OR math! Why do we even have to do homework?" "Oh no, not again!" thought Katie's mother. She couldn't bear the idea of yet another evening filled with tension, anger, and frustration around the one thing that was supposed to make her daughter smarter – homework.

For some parents, this situation is all too familiar. For others, friction over homework may ensue only on occasion; and for the lucky few, homework requires little parental involvement. This book is for parents who have experienced stress, self-doubt, and anxiety over homework. It is for those who wonder if there is a better, easier way to help their children experience greater success in those precious after-school hours. And it is also for those who want to set up a good foundation for smooth sailing in later years.

How Parents Can Help

Whether you like it or not, you are drawn into your child's homework battles and victories. On good nights, a sense of achievement and relief fills the air when the work is finally done. On the other evenings, you truly wonder how your relationship with your child can survive another round of grueling conflict. Why is homework time so contentious? The problem is that while parents understand the value of academics, their children rarely do. The good news is that homework does not have to be so darned hard. There are many practical interventions that you can put in place that will relieve the angst and foster accomplishment. These solutions can make a real difference in your child's view of homework, your sanity, and more importantly, the relationship you have with your child.

However, if you want to make homework simpler and less stressful, you should be willing to do hard work up front. Setting a basic foundation that includes routines, consistent expectations, and just the right study tools for your child's unique needs is imperative. When students of all ages know what to expect from day to day, homework time is much easier. In addition, studies have shown that a parent's attitude towards schoolwork is contagious. Parents can make a difference in how their children perceive homework when the parents are supportive of the teacher's requests and convey that the additional practice gained from completing homework is an important part of the learning process.

Other research has demonstrated that when parents model the skills they are trying to teach, such as organization and time management, and of course, a positive attitude, they are taking a big step in the right direction. Children learn more by observing an adult demonstrating these skills than by being told what to do. This is especially the case when it comes to homework.

Now that you know that you can help with homework, let's get started! Although you might be tempted to skip through the following chapters to move on to Part II of this book – **_please, don't do it_**. Chapters 1, 2, and 3 are must-reads, as they lay the foundation for long-term homework success. Jumping ahead to the profile chapters (Procrastinator, Rusher, etc.) without this foundation is like trying to eat a pizza without the crust. It's simply too messy and destroys the experience. No matter what you do, the missing ingredient will always be the crust. The next few chapters will provide you with the information you need to make Chapters 4 through 9 work. The right crust can make all the difference!

Chapter 1

Homework: What Is The REAL Problem?

Goals

In this chapter you will learn:

- Why homework is harder for some students.

- How executive functioning impacts academic performance.

- About the underlying issues that cause difficulties.

- To identify skill deficits in reading and writing that impact homework.

- How attention significantly affects learning.

Another night of frustration and anger has ended in the Robertson family. James, a bright-eyed sixth grader, has dawdled his way through two hours of homework that should have taken no more than an hour. Desperate to get him back on track and to merely finish the work, his mom threatened him with being grounded for a week. When that didn't get him going, she bribed him with the possibility of having his friends spend the night over the weekend. Neither approach worked. James procrastinated until he ran out of excuses.

Upon starting his math homework, he couldn't seem to recall exactly how to solve the problems. He became so frustrated that he scribbled a few numbers on his paper and shoved it randomly into his backpack, just to get it "out of sight and out of mind." Knowing that James couldn't have completed the work in such a short time, his mom inquired about it, only to ignite a heated battle. James wanted nothing to do with his mother's requests to check his work. The next 20 minutes were wasted on an argument like all the others before in which nothing was ever resolved.

His mother wondered what was going on with her son. Questions filled her head —"Is it me? Am I a bad parent? Could James have other problems?"

A Parent's Role In The Battle Over Homework

James' mother could not get her head around the reasons for her son's resistance. She thought that perhaps part of his problem might be due to his weak study skills or the way she handled him. If only she could find a way to end the homework battles.

A myriad of studies on homework have been conducted over the years. By and large, they show that households with structure and routines have kids who are more academically successful. Having clear expectations for behavior and implementing carefully chosen incentives and consequences is of the utmost importance. Clearly, valuing education, hard work, and a positive attitude can help your child to become an integral member of the school community. So yes, it's true that parenting style is a clear indicator of success in and out of the classroom. But what if you run a supportive, loving, and structured household and still have a child who struggles terribly with homework? There could be other issues at play.

Mr. and Mrs. Robertson realized that trying to "fix" James wasn't working. After many years of nightly arguments similar to this one, his parents recognized they had to be proactive, not reactive. They altered their approach and positive changes followed. James fell in line and required less handholding, but the battle was not won. James' behavior improved, but he continued to stumble academically. After consultations with education professionals, his parents finally discovered that James' academic issues were tied to weak executive function skills. This and the following chapter will help you to better understand how even the slightest underlying difficulty can affect homework completion.

Why Homework Is So Hard For Some Kids

For a number of students, homework is a very natural process. Mom and Dad do not need to intervene often, if at all, and the homework is done efficiently and returned to school. For other students, though, homework is a very difficult and painful task. Stories of heated arguments, tears, missing assignments, and poor grades are not unusual.

Parents are often baffled at how regularly their children fight them on homework. They can't understand why one of their kids has tremendous difficulty bringing the right materials home, getting started, and completing the most basic assignment when the other can easily persevere through tough tasks. How can two children with the same parents have such different experiences when it comes to homework? It's likely that these children come to the table with different sets of innate abilities. It is also possible that there are problems lurking below the surface. When parents understand these difficulties, they are better able to help their children tackle homework obstacles.

Executive Functions – The Crucial Element For Homework Success

Over the last 20 years, an increasing amount of research has examined mental processes controlled in the frontal lobes of the brain. These cognitive processes are called executive functions, an umbrella term for the skills involved in mental control and self-regulation. Examples of these skills are the ability to strategize, plan ahead, organize, and recall information.

Some individuals have very well developed executive function skills, while others, like James, do not. Although poor executive function ability is not a clinical diagnosis, it does help to explain why some kids seem to naturally have it together in these areas more than others.

As you can imagine, strong executive function abilities are vital for school success. In the realm of homework, a student with these skills can:

- Come home from school and determine when homework must start and finish in time for the day's extracurricular activities.

- Prioritize assignments.

- Organize materials based on what is needed for the task at hand.

- Get started independently.

- Sustain effort to get the work done, even when it's challenging.

- Complete one assignment and move on to another without a hitch.

- Put the work in the appropriate folders upon completion.

On the other hand, a student with weak Executive Function skills often:

- Has no plan before starting homework; regularly begins with the first assignment that comes to mind.

- Cannot find the correct books, worksheets, or notes that are needed for the assignment. Sometimes, they have been left behind at school.

- Isn't sure how to get started and feels easily overwhelmed.

- Gets easily distracted and feels fatigued, especially if the work is challenging.

- Struggles to get work completed in a timely manner.

- Puts finished homework randomly into books or binders and has a hard time finding it the next day at school when the teacher calls for it.

Let's take a look at a seventh grader named Jill, who has struggled for years with poor executive function skills. Even though her difficulties are very different from James', both households are equally burdened by constant tension and exasperation.

Jill is the quintessential social butterfly. She's a collector of friends and has a gift for making conversation with those she's met for the first time, even adults. Although Jill thrives in the social arena, school has been a huge disappointment for her. She comes from a nurturing and supportive family, one that highly values education and personal responsibility. Her older sister, Karen, is an academic superstar, and her younger sibling, Sophia, manages to keep a solid B average. Jill's parents are hard working, accomplished adults, but for Jill, school has been nothing more than a lesson in frustration.

Interestingly, Jill scores well on standardized tests, so to her parents and teachers, her lack of success is perplexing. They wonder if she is simply lazy, but that theory doesn't hold water. Jill does care about her grades, but forgets to write down the assignments from the board and leaves important materials at school. In seventh grade, her teachers expect her to maintain organized folders and a locker. They don't have the time to sit down with her on an individual basis to help with these skills. Jill keeps falling further behind, not because she isn't capable, but because she cannot stay on top of her schoolwork.

It's easy to see that Jill is certainly at the lower end of the scale when it comes to executive functioning. Her sister, Karen, who is efficient, methodical, and organized, is at the high end, and Sophia is most likely in the middle. Will Jill ever be like Karen? No, it is unlikely, but with direct instruction in planning, organization, and study skills, Jill will be able to move closer to the middle.

Attention Issues – A Common Cause Of Frustration

In addition to the problems seen with executive functions, children may have other attention issues which may also affect their performance in school and at home. These children may be diagnosed with ADHD (Attention Deficit Hyperactivity Disorder) and may exhibit hyperactivity, inattentiveness, or a bit of both. Not all individuals with weak executive function skills have ADHD, but all of those with ADHD have difficulty with executive function skills.

I wish I had a dollar for every parent who said, "He doesn't have an attention problem. He can surf the web for three hours straight!" While this may be accurate, the true test of attention is being able to regulate it as needed, not to merely focus. Anyone can attend for long periods of time to a task they love – video games, for example. But being able to sustain effort related to an unpleasant task, such as homework, is the real test.

Most individuals can force themselves to focus long enough to complete something they don't want to do. However, when a person cannot make himself do it, no matter how hard he tries, he may be struggling with a greater problem such as ADHD. Some children are so impacted that they are stuck in their tracks. Others are only mildly inattentive and compensate fairly well.

Whether your child has a diagnosis of ADHD or not, difficulty regulating attention can take its toll in the classroom. A child with attention issues may have trouble in the following core academic areas:

Reading Comprehension

- Reads words without gaining a deep understanding of the text
- Cannot remember the key points after reading a page
- Often has to reread
- Confuses main ideas with details

Writing

- Has difficultly editing and proofreading
- Thoughts are not organized; there is no clear beginning, middle, and end
- Easily drained; must juggle correct grammar, punctuation, and spelling, all while composing an organized piece

Math

- Loses track of problems requiring multiple steps, such as long division and involved algebraic equations
- Struggles with attention to detail, such as operational signs or positive and negative numbers

Children and adolescents cannot create change by simply "trying harder," "focusing more," or "controlling themselves." If they could, they would. These students need support systems at home and at school.

If this sounds like your child, your support may need to be on two fronts – helping with the content itself and introducing learning strategies. When assisting with content, you may need to periodically review the concepts or details that your child could have missed out on in class. It's likely that he may not be absorbing all the information due to distractibility. Sometimes, homework may be a battle because your child does not have the information to do the work. Be sure that he understands how to solve the problems or answer the questions before he begins.

Children with attention problems benefit tremendously from strategies to help themselves stay on track. In Chapters 4 through 9, I will provide you with tips to address this common problem. For example, the use of a timer, break menu, cuing system, and self-monitoring techniques are described in detail. In addition, the active reading and highlighting strategies contained in Chapter 10 are essential study skills to help your child learn and retain information.

Could There Be A Skill Deficit?

The roots of homework woes vary. Some families find that simply by tweaking a few parts of their after-school routine, they see significant changes.

Sometimes children struggle with subjects because, for one reason or another, they have not acquired core academic skills. Once this deficit is known, it can usually be remediated with new and different instructional techniques and extra practice. For other children, problems run deeper. A small percentage of children have learning disabilities that, if not identified, will preclude appropriate interventions. Whether diagnosed or not, the following information assists parents in understanding how these issues impact school and homework performance.

Reading Issues

Difficulties with reading have a widespread effect on a student's academic performance. Students who have trouble reading often also struggle in social studies and science or in any subject that requires reading. These kids come to dread school because it requires mastery of skills many people take for granted. Reading requires intense mental fortitude as students must:

- Sound out unfamiliar words while remembering what has already been read.

- Understand words and grammar.

- Build ideas and images.

- Compare new ideas to what is already known.

- Store information into memory.

Researchers have discovered that many youngsters' problems begin early on when they have specific trouble sounding out words. Interestingly, these children often fly under the radar because they are bright and become expert memorizers. They learn to read not by sounding out (decoding), but by memorizing. In the early years, this might not be detected because they seem to be reading, but they are not. As the words become longer, these children cannot get by with just memorization. Unfortunately, without decoding skills to fall back on, they become easily frustrated and before long they lag behind their peers.

Sometimes, students who read fluently still falter because they fail to comprehend what they have read. These students often have a hard time separating main ideas from details and cannot make connections to the text. They often complain that they've read to the bottom of the page and can't recall the information.

If you suspect that this may be the case with your child, touch base with the school or consult with a local tutor who specializes in reading remediation. Keep in mind that resolving this issue alone will have a significant positive impact on homework completion.

Writing Troubles

In my practice, we often see students who have a great deal of difficulty with organizing and producing written language. These students are typically very verbal, but just can't get their thoughts down on paper accurately. Writing is a taxing subject; just like a juggler, a writer must keep many balls in the air at the same time. He must coordinate his ideas with the correct vocabulary, grammar, spelling, and punctuation. Because writing is an integral part of each and every subject, children who resist it are going to have a harder time with homework. These students often fare much better when they are able to type their work instead of writing it by hand. In addition, utilizing software, such as the programs detailed on page 236, can change resistance into enthusiasm.

Emotional Problems

Anxiety, depression, and other mental health issues can also seriously affect homework. Any of these problems can cause students to avoid assignments, perform poorly on tests, and have low self-esteem and confidence. Students may feel that they are not capable of doing well, so they reason, "Why should I try?" If you observe a pattern of academic malaise or a sharp downward spiral, seek out an experienced therapist who can pinpoint the problem and put you and your child on the right path.

The bottom line for all parents is to trust your instincts—you know your child best. This book will offer strategies to help you manage common homework obstacles. However, if the issues you face become bigger than just having a "bad day" here or there, consider a professional evaluation. Even the mildest learning, attention, or emotional problem can be very painful to the student experiencing it, and what starts out as minor can become a serious issue later on. When in doubt, seek an outside opinion.

Chapter 2

How Parenting Styles Affect Homework

Goals

In this chapter you will learn:

- To identify your parenting style.

- What research says is the most successful way to parent.

- How to modify your current style.

- How to set up after-school structure and routines.

- How a parent's role changes as children age.

Just as students come to the table with different sets of skills and capabilities, their parents do as well. Some parents have a knack for establishing expectations, routines, and structure. Others find this challenging. In this chapter, you will learn about parenting styles that correlate with homework success. Researchers have found that parenting style has a significant influence on a child's overall success in life.

Parenting Styles And Why They Matter

It has been my experience that parents who are the most effective at helping their children with homework are those considered to be **authoritative** parents. According to researchers in the field of child development, **authoritative** parents take a balanced approach – they are both demanding and responsive. They create and monitor clear standards and expectations for their children's conduct. They discipline in an assertive and supportive manner, and want their children to be assertive as well. Yet they also respond to their children's needs when appropriate. These parents are more open to a natural give and take with their children. So often their children are happy, competent, and academically successful.

On the other hand, parents in an **authoritarian** household are overly demanding, and insist on making most or all of the decisions for the child. They show little trust for their child and appear heavy-handed. They discourage open communication with the attitude of "it's my way or the highway." These parents may hold unrealistically high expectations for grades, without providing the support necessary for academic success. When these grades aren't achieved, punishment is usually the answer. Although this approach may lead to obedient behavior in the short-term, children reared by **authoritarian** parents report greater feelings of unhappiness, low self-esteem, and problems maintaining friendships.

Permissive parents err in the opposite direction. They have difficulty establishing boundaries and limits. They deeply love their children, but often relate to them as friends or peers. Rules regarding homework are nonexistent or inconsistent at best. **Permissive** parenting frequently results in children who have difficulty regulating their own behavior. They encounter problems with authority and rank lower in happiness and academic achievement.

Lastly, **uninvolved** parents provide for their child's basic needs, but are emotionally detached. Children raised by **uninvolved** parents rank lowest in all areas of success and happiness. They often lack self-control, feel poorly about themselves, and have difficulty creating and maintaining personal relationships.

For a better idea of each parenting style, let's look at how each type would respond to the following scenario.

Donna is an average student, but to her, homework is drudgery. She simply doesn't want to engage in the process of getting started.

The Permissive Parent

The Uninvolved Parent

The Authoritarian Parent

The Authoritative Parent

About Authoritative Parenting

In the sketch on page twenty seven, Donna was given a choice. Because she had a history of procrastinating, her mother tied the time at which she began homework to a privilege – Donna's cell phone. She gave her a choice between starting on time and earning phone usage, or not beginning on time and losing access to her phone for the evening. Another option would have been to allow Donna the choice between a couple of start times, but to hold firm on the end time. She and her parents may agree that all homework must be done by 8 pm. Although Donna would have the option of when to begin, the 8 pm cutoff would be non-negotiable. When kids have a say in decisions, compliance is less likely to be an issue.

With the authoritative parenting style, choices are provided so that the child has decision-making power, but important rules are non-negotiable. In addition, the reasoning behind rules is discussed with the child, so that she is well aware why the particular homework policy has been implemented. Researchers have found that children raised by authoritative parents generally have the following outcomes:

- They accept failures and successes more readily. Since these children had parents who helped them work through trying times, these students were more able to face roadblocks with maturity, and successes with exuberance.

- They are self-reliant. Children reported feeling a sense of control over their lives, and were better able to articulate and assert their goals and beliefs. They felt confident about their abilities to achieve tasks and were independently motivated to begin tackling those tasks on their own.

- They are happy and have a lively disposition. Being treated by parents in a warm and democratic manner makes these children more apt to treat themselves and others with warmth, too. They've developed positive attitudes about themselves, school, and peers. These students are well-liked by teachers and peers and have a higher grade point average.

- They regulate their emotions and behaviors better. These independent-minded children understand that throwing temper tantrums isn't the way to get attention. They manage their ups and downs with grace and know appropriate social conventions and cues.

Moreover, the presence of an authoritative parent is one of the most consistent predictors of a child's future competence from early childhood through adolescence. The benefits of this approach are clear, and much of what you'll learn in the following chapters is based on the authoritative parenting style. Some of these strategies may feel uncomfortable to you at first, but give them a try.

Examples Of Authoritative Parenting

The following scenarios give practical examples of how the authoritative parent deals with homework.

Stephanie and Weekend Homework

Stephanie has a homework assignment that is due on Monday, but it is Friday, and she wants to relax. Her family has a banquet to attend on Sunday at 5 pm; therefore, it must be done beforehand. Stephanie is fixated on going to the movies with her friends on Saturday night. Her parents request that the work be done before she ventures off to the movie theatre, however, they allow her to determine when she'll do it.

This authoritative approach gives both parties some control and it gives Stephanie a chance to practice her time management skills. Stephanie's parents trust that she'll have the work done before leaving, but they verify her claim by asking to see it. If she doesn't have it done, her parents will not allow her to leave – no negotiation. A critical authoritative skill that Stephanie's parents exhibit is the ability to provide a choice (when she does the assignment) balanced by a reward (going to the movies) and a consequence (not going to the movies).

Matt and His Mom

Matt's mom is a single working parent, but she always takes the time to attend school functions and stay apprised of Matt's grades. Lately, Matt, generally a good eighth grade student, has been claiming that he has finished his homework at school, so there is nothing to bring home. His mother is rightfully suspicious, so she went online to check his grades. Lo and behold, he has missing assignments. Mom has an open discussion with Matt about his work habits, wherein he admits to slacking off to spend more time with his friends. Instead of punishing her son, Mom does three things:

- *She asks to see Matt's planner. Although she trusts that her son has recorded his schoolwork accurately, she verifies this periodically by asking him to pull up the teacher's assignments that are posted online.*

- *She and Matt agree that this will be done for three weeks. If Matt has been diligent during that time, his mom will back off, only checking in once or twice per week. She agrees not to intervene on the other days. It is his responsibility to get the work done.*

- *Mom gives her son choices about homework completion. She insists that it be finished before he goes outside to play, but allows him to choose the time at which he'll start his work. By giving Matt options, she puts the ball in his court.*

Matt's mother is a pro at utilizing "trust, but verify," a skill that authoritative parents possess. She doesn't micromanage the situation by emailing his teachers or by calling other parents daily to be sure he wrote down the work in his planner correctly. She expects that he is honest, but she is experienced enough to know that Matt has a tendency to cut corners if he thinks no one is watching. So, she verifies a few times each week by asking him to log on to the school's website and show her the homework his teachers have posted.

Chris, Mark, and Molly – Squabbling Siblings

Chris, Mark, and Molly, ages 9, 13, and 14 are constantly bickering when they should be doing their homework. The children's step-father, Joe, realizes that their behavior is sidetracking their schoolwork. Instead of having the permissive attitude "kids will be kids" and walking away or holding onto authoritarian beliefs that they should be abruptly punished, Joe takes appropriate action. He asks the kids where they can work quietly without disturbing each other. He helps them to set up separate study areas. Joe and the kids agree that all three will have "lights out" 20 minutes earlier if they continue squabbling, but that as a group, they can earn a later bedtime of 20 minutes by cooperating. In addition, Joe agrees to give a warning about their behavior. If they aren't able to work quietly and independently after he calmly says, "This is your warning," they earn an earlier lights out.

Joe's style is authoritative in nature because he allows the children to solve their argument on their own before he intervenes. Again, a choice is given – work it out and earn a later bedtime or continue arguing and get an earlier bedtime. Now, they are in control of the outcome.

Change Your Parenting Role Depending On Your Child's Age

Authoritative parents also understand that their roles change as the years pass. In the primary grades (kindergarten through third), there is more handholding and oversight during homework time. Young children, just beginning to be assigned homework, need much more parental involvement than older students simply because they do not possess internal structure and study habits. Authoritative parents feel it is their role to lay the foundation early on, so that their children will be independent learners as they age. During the middle and high school years, students are expected to put academics first, but they continue to need guidance. Authoritative parents do not dictate when, where, and how their children do their homework, instead they have a general expectation of work before play. In these households, parents see their role as the occasional coach, not as the tutor or friend.

In the elementary grades, parents are very much a part of the homework process by:

- Setting up a daily routine.

- Agreeing upon a starting time and location.

- Creating the expectation that they want to know what is on tap for the evening and check homework for completion once it's finished.

- Making sure that completed homework goes into the backpack.

But as the child ages, a more hands-off approach is appropriate. Homework is discussed and loosely monitored, but supervision and attention to detail isn't warranted.

Parenting Style And Lifetime Achievement

Parenting style is not only important for school success, but for lifetime achievement. A recent study published in *The Leadership Quarterly* found that children raised in authoritative households were more likely to become leaders at work and in their communities later in life. The researchers found that a firm parenting approach that allowed children to test the rules and learn from their mistakes correlated with leadership as adults. Interestingly, this study suggests that leaders are raised more than they are born.

Chapter 3

When It Comes To Homework – What Works For All Kids

Goals

In this chapter you will learn:

- Why certain parenting principles apply to ALL children and adolescents.

- How to set expectations, time, and place for homework completion.

- How to effectively praise your child to increase his perseverance.

- To eliminate idle threats and replace them with choices.

- How family dinners improve grades.

- How to find the balance between helping too much and not enough.

This chapter is a must read for any parent with school-aged children and adolescents!

Carolina - BEFORE

After a long day at school, Carolina Juarez can't wait to wind down by watching her favorite television show and texting her friends. She arrives home at 3 pm and spends the next hour engaged in anything electronic. Her attention shifts from the television to texting, and to the computer, even though it should be on her homework. At 4:30 pm her mother, Marta, arrives home from work. Today,

Marta calmly inquires about Carolina's assignments. Her tranquil approach is far different from her volatile reaction yesterday when she realized Carolina had not yet even touched her schoolwork. Carolina takes out her books, but realizes that she must get ready for her 5 pm ballet class or she'll be late.

Carolina returns home from ballet at 7 pm, finally getting a chance to eat dinner. She glances at her planner to determine what needs to be done for tomorrow and discovers she has a science fair project due in just two days. Since it's not an immediate concern, she only focuses on tonight's work in algebra and history.

Carolina feels she is quite adept at multitasking, so she gets some work done while watching television and talking on the phone with her friends. At 9 pm, Carolina's father yells at her to turn off the television and to get to work, but now she can't remember quite how to solve those algebra problems. An hour later, her father is furious to find Carolina chatting on her cell phone with only two of twenty algebra problems completed.

How could Carolina and her parents gain control over homework instead of letting it control them? Read on to learn about what will not only work for Carolina, but for every child in your home.

The Foundation for Success

Laying the groundwork for stress-free homework involves setting up basic parameters. Whether you have a Procrastinator, a Rusher, or a Disorganized child or teen living in your home, certain parenting strategies and techniques work for all kids. Regardless of age or ability, children need and crave routine, consistent discipline, and fair expectations. They need their parents to be involved in school life, but not to micromanage all of their activities. They also need praise for a job well done and the privileges and rewards that go along with it. To assure less drama and homework free of hassles, take a look at the three rules found in this chapter.

RULE # 1 – ESTABLISH ROUTINES IN YOUR HOME AND FAMILY LIFE.

RULE #2 – TALK SO YOUR CHILD WILL LISTEN.

RULE #3 – CARVE OUT TIME FOR FAMILY MEETINGS AND DINNERS.

Rule # 1

ESTABLISH ROUTINES IN YOUR HOME AND FAMILY LIFE.

Time after time, research has documented the benefits of after-school routines. Children who are expected to start homework at a given time, have a quiet place to study, and are reinforced positively by their caregivers do far better than those with little to no structure. So, what does a routine look like?

Same Time

Most students, regardless of age, need some downtime after school. About a half hour is usually enough time to grab a snack and relax, but it's not enough time to become overly involved in another activity. Although each day is not the same due to sports and other extracurricular activities, try to identify a daily start time. There are essentially three times your child can start homework: right after school, before dinner, or after dinner.

You may find that the time at which your child begins homework changes as he gets older. Elementary school aged children are often fresher after school and do well beginning work right after a short break; however, many adolescents like to start homework either before or after dinner. Beginning homework too close to bedtime is generally not a good idea, no matter what the age.

If you feel like you've tried to secure a daily schedule before without success, put the list in writing and for even more reinforcement, color code it. Visual reminders are far superior to verbal ones and also allow students to adhere to a routine more independently. Review the schedule and post it in a prominent place (the refrigerator, homework area, or desk). Try using a simple schedule like this one for young children. Often, seeing a day at a time is less overwhelming than a week-at-a-glance.

Examples Of After-School Schedules

At Home Parent	Working Parent
3:00 Break	5:30 Arrive Home And Break
3:30 Homework	6:00 Begin Homework
4:30 Free Time	6:30 Dinner
6:30 Dinner	7:00 Homework
7:00 Chores	7:30 Chores
7:30 Privileges	8:00 Privileges
9:00 Bedtime	9:00 Bedtime

Older students do well with a weekly schedule similar to the one below.

Weekly Schedule				For the week of 10-5	
Time	Mon	Tue	Wed	Thur	Fri/Sat/Sun (choose one)
3:30-4:00	break	break	break	break	
4:00-4:30	HW	soccer	break	soccer	
4:30-5:00	HW		HW		
5:00-5:30	religion				
5:30-6:00	religion	↓	↓	↓	
6:00-6:30	HW	HW	free time	HW	HW
6:30-7:00	dinner	dinner	dinner	dinner	HW
7:00-7:30	chores	HW	chores	chores	
7:30-8:00	free time	↓	free time	HW	
8:00-9:00	↓	chores free time	↓	↓	
9:00-9:30	read in bed	read in bed	read in bed	read in bed	
9:30	lights out	lights out	lights out	lights out	

Same Place

Kids like choice, and allowing them a couple of options for a homework location is a good idea. Be sure that the area is generally quiet without access to electronics (cell phone, television, video games, etc.) or other distracting activities. Stock this area with materials needed for homework completion.

Same Expectations

Even though most students would love the excitement of every day being a different adventure, the fact is that they need consistent parental expectations. This means that homework must be completed before privileges are granted. Before access to video games, time with friends, or cell phone use, ask to see the completed homework. This simple expectation eliminates a whole lot of fighting late at night because play has come before work.

Rule # 2

TALK SO YOUR CHILD WILL LISTEN

Over the years, I've worked with families facing all kinds of difficult homework issues. Those who have been successful in eliminating these problems have done two things – they've gone from parenting reactively to proactively, and more importantly, they have opened up the lines of communication within their households.

Plan Ahead Before a Problem Arises

Being proactive instead of reactive can transform the parent/child relationship from one weighted down with tension to one full of peace. Why is proactive parenting so important? It's simple—when parents are thinking ahead, they anticipate trouble spots and head them off. These parents have clear rules and stick to them. The result is that kids understand the rules and consequences, and exhibit more on-target behaviors.

On the other hand, a reactive parent responds emotionally when a negative behavior occurs and the response most likely varies from one day to the next. Sometimes the student's behavior evokes no response and sometimes there's a fire storm. It's no wonder the child becomes confused!

Let's take a look at Carolina's situation described earlier in this chapter. Clearly, one of the struggles her parents have is getting her to start and complete homework on time. Using the rules set out in this chapter to overcome this dilemma, they would begin by restricting Carolina's access to anything with a screen (television, cell phone, computer, etc.) until the work is done. This may come as a shock to Carolina, but not only are these tangible items contributing to battles between her and her parents, they are also impacting her academic progress. Once she can prove that all of her assignments are complete, her parents should praise her effort and perseverance, and grant her the earned privileges.

The following scenarios contain examples of common challenges and solutions. In each case, the parent thinks ahead and uses the right language with the child in order to help solve the potential conflict.

Do these scenarios ring a bell?

Challenge	Solution
Callie announces that she's completed her homework – in record time again, only 10 minutes! Knowing that others spend about an hour, her father sends her to her room to "think about the consequences of her actions."	Ask to see Callie's assignment list before she begins her homework. Briefly discuss what a good finished product will look like. When completed, be sure Callie shares her completed work with an adult.
Sarah is so fearful of doing her homework incorrectly that she insists on one of her parents sitting next to her. After many arguments over the situation, her father declares, "Enough is enough! We won't hold your hand anymore!"	Instead of a drastic reduction, cut back the usual 45 minutes of assistance gradually by five minutes each night, until help is given just to get started. Because the problem didn't pop up overnight, a cold turkey approach will likely be ineffective.
Teri forgot her Civics book at school once again. Knowing that she has a major project due, her mother drives to the campus and retrieves the book for her.	Recognize that it's the child's job to bring home materials. Help Teri create a "things to bring home" section in her planner. When homework is given, Teri can jot down the materials needed.

Praise Successfully

Praise is a powerful tool, especially when it comes to homework. Research shows that by simply praising effort rather than intelligence, kids will develop greater motivation to keep trying, even when the going gets tough.

Dr. Carol Dweck conducted a landmark study on the effects of praise on 400 fifth graders. One at a time, the children were given a fairly easy, non-verbal IQ test. After randomly dividing the children, some were praised for their intelligence ("You must be smart at this") and the others were praised for their effort ("You must have worked really hard").

Later in the testing session, the same children were given a choice of tests. They were told that they could choose a more difficult test than the first one, but that they'd learn a lot from this type of test, or they could choose an easy test, very similar to the first one. Results indicated that the type of praise they received after the initial test significantly affected their decisions on repeat testing. Ninety percent of the students commended for their effort chose the more difficult task. The majority of those praised for intelligence chose the easy test. The "smart" kids took the easy way out. Why did Dr. Dweck think this happened? She stated, "When we praise children for their intelligence, we tell them that this is the name of the game: Look smart and don't risk making mistakes."

In another round of testing, none of the students had a choice. Each child was administered an assessment two years ahead of their grade level and every child failed. However, their approach to the test varied significantly. Those who were praised for their effort "got very involved, willing to try every solution to the puzzles." The students praised for their intelligence gave up easily and looked "miserable." Finally, after having induced failure, Dweck gave another test similar to the very first easy one. Remarkably, the children that had been praised for effort improved on their first score by about 30 percent, but those who were told they were smart did worse. Their scores declined by 20 percent.

Dr. Dweck stated, "Simply emphasizing effort gives a child a variable they can control. They come to see themselves as in control of their own success." This affects homework because kids who feel in control are more likely to exert greater effort to get their work done well. They are more likely to persevere in the face of difficulty.

Numerous other studies have found that specific praise is far superior to non-specific overtures. When words are too general, children discount their parents' good intentions altogether, not feeling that their words are sincere. Given that praise needs to be specific and focused on effort, here's how to make the transformation in your home.

The Praise Makeover

Before	After
"Great job!"	"I like the way you kept trying even when the problems became harder."
"I'm proud of you!"	"You went back to check your work-- that extra step was a great idea."
"You got an A!"	"Those extra practice problems you did really made a difference!"
"You're so smart!"	"The ideas you thought of are unique. Where did you learn about that?"

The Praise Makeover

Before	After
"Are you the best reader in your class?"	"You really understand what you read! Going back to look up the answers to the questions helps with remembering."
"You're really good at math!"	"All that hard work on your math homework really paid off."

One last thought about praise – use it in a 2:1 ratio. For every suggestion for improvement, start with praise and end with praise. Let's say your son brings you his spelling assignment and there are clearly a few mistakes.

Instead of	Try
"You need to correct #2."	"You spelled 'presidential' correctly and that's a tough word! I just see that you need to correct #2, but overall you worked hard to write neatly."

Outcome:

This time around, he will be much more likely to correct the work without a fight and feel good about the work he did well.

Instead of	Try
"I can barely read this!"	"You spelled the difficult words correctly. The last two sentences are hard to read because the words aren't on lines. Correct those, but I see that you're really working hard to master your spelling list."

Outcome:

By insisting that the last two sentences be rewritten, the parent is reinforcing good handwriting. Some parents would insist on the whole assignment being redone, but this approach leaves the child feeling the task is insurmountable. In this scenario, the parent sandwiched constructive criticism between positive comments, increasing the chance that his son will be willing to seek him out for assistance in the future.

Eliminate Idle Threats

Let's face it – homework can bring out the worst in even the best parent. How many times have you wanted to say, "I've had it with you...I can't take this anymore! You're on restriction for the rest of the month!" It's easy to get to the end of your rope and make rash remarks out of frustration and desperation. Not only can threats be hurtful to kids, they can cause parental guilt. The biggest problem with idle threats is that parents relent without following through on their words. When this occurs, children develop an awareness that Mom and Dad don't mean what they say. Their reasoning goes like this – "Mom and Dad always give in. Restriction will probably be for only a couple of days, not an entire month, that's not so bad. I can do it again without really being punished."

Idle threats diminish a parent's credibility. Instead, develop a rule and consistently implement it. For example, if your rule is no video game usage until homework is done, institute a reward (games are available when all work is complete) and a consequence (no games for the rest of the day if you choose to play before work is done). In order to make the rule work, it's important to impose the reward and consequence each day. This way, your child knows you stand behind your word. When you consistently mean what you say, your child will beg and plead a whole lot less because he knows you'll hold your ground.

Instead of This	Say This
"If you don't have your reading done by 5 pm, you're not going to chess club – end of discussion."	*"Your reading must be done by 5 pm in order to go to chess club. I'll give you a warning at 4:45."*
"If you complain one more time about finishing that math assignment, you'll be grounded for two weeks."	*"One of our rules is no complaining during homework. We've agreed that I'll give you two warnings. This is the first warning. If you still complain after the second, there will be no computer time tonight."*
"I better not get another email from your teacher about a missing assignment. If I do, you're off the lacrosse team for the rest of the season."	*"Your English teacher sent an email about a missing assignment. Let's discuss why it's late. I'll check your planner for the next three weeks. If more than two assignments are late or missing, you'll be restricted from video games for one week."*

Instead of This	Say This
"Your father and I will not tolerate another C on your report card. If your interim grade isn't a B or better, you'll lose access to every electronic device in this house."	*"I see that you earned a C in math. Let's talk about the reasons behind it. Before you go to chorus practice on Tuesdays and Thursdays, let's review your homework and prepare for any upcoming tests. Once I know you're on the right track, we'll only touch base on Thursdays."*

Give a Warning Before Consequences

Giving a child a warning before enforcing a consequence allows him to correct his behavior. Be calm and matter of fact – "This is your warning. If you continue to doodle instead of completing your worksheet, then bedtime is at 8:45 instead of 9 pm." Say no more. If your child generally responds after one warning, you're golden. Some children need two and even three warnings. In advance, agree that you'll always give a certain number of warnings to help get your child back on track. Stick to that number. State that you are giving a warning and then walk away. At any point when you see that he's doing the right thing, praise his diligence. By giving warnings and positively reinforcing on task behavior, constant reminders will be gone for good.

Remain Neutral

We've all heard the term "helicopter parent" and pray we're not one. A helicopter parent is one who is overly involved in every aspect of his or her child's life, especially school. These well-meaning parents are determined to make learning such a positive experience that they refuse to allow failure. The problem with this approach is that kids don't learn to be resilient. What happens when they get a bad grade, forget a book at school, or have a conflict with a teacher? When Mom and Dad swoop in, quizzing relentlessly to improve the grade, running back to school to retrieve the book, or blaming the teacher, they are depriving the child of a valuable learning opportunity. The ability to learn from adversity and deal with tough problems are signs of maturity and optimism. Conflict is a natural part of life.

Successful parents are involved, but not overly so. They take a keen interest in the lives of their children by attending parent conferences, checking over homework, and supporting teachers' decisions. They understand that they are there as a homework coach, to help when necessary, but not to correct every answer or insist on unrealistic grades. Remaining neutrally involved is important to help your child become an independent and motivated learner.

Rule # 3
CARVE OUT TIME FOR FAMILY MEETINGS AND DINNERS

Hold Family Meetings

Many families have found that weekly, biweekly, or monthly family meetings are excellent ways of opening the lines of communication. Taking just 20 minutes to discuss family rules, expectations, and privileges goes a long way in helping children, especially adolescents, feel their voices are heard. Here's how it works:

- Set a standing date, such as during or after dinner. Make it a pleasant experience – serve dessert and don't allow any interruptions, such as phone calls.

- A parent is the chairperson and the scribe. He or she makes sure everyone gets a turn to share their thoughts without interruption.

- One person shares a problem they want to solve.

- Solutions are proposed and discussed.

- The final resolution is written in the Family Meeting Journal.

Family Journal

October 10
Homework Policies

- Homework must be finished before playing with friends, except on Friday.

- Weekend homework can be done anytime before dinner on Sunday.

- Friends can come over when homework is done, but not before.

If you're unsure how to begin, choose a topic. For example, you may start by saying "Tonight, let's talk about friends coming over after school. I think we should have a policy about playing outside only when homework is done."

Just like adults, children are more likely to follow rules or policies if they feel they either came up with the idea or contributed to it. The family meeting teaches problem solving and respect for others' ideas, even to the youngest participants.

Have Family Dinners

Believe it or not, your family's eating habits can have a profound effect on your child's academic success. The routine of preparing and sharing meals regularly creates a sense of unity. Though the hustle and bustle of everyday life can get in the way, it's important to carve out time specifically to sit down together around the table. Students who eat with their families on a consistent basis are:

- 40 percent more likely to earn mainly As and Bs in school.

- Less likely to smoke, drink, do drugs, get depressed, develop eating disorders, or contemplate suicide.

- More apt to believe their parents are proud of them.

Like anything else, though, eating dinners together does take practice. The less often a family meets to share a meal, the worse the experience is bound to be. So, plan on as many meals together as possible, even if you serve take out or only have a limited time available. Some things you might want to consider when getting ready are:

- Turn off the TV. It prohibits meaningful conversation.

- Use dinnertime to tell your child why he's a great kid.

- Focus on the positives during dinners.

- Refrain from discussing shortcomings or unfulfilled responsibilities.

If you are the parent of an adolescent, it is even more critical to engage in family dinners. Teens can be resistant to participating in anything family oriented, but don't give up. Older students may say that they are too busy, would prefer to eat with friends, or don't like the food being served, but in reality they long for spending time with Mom, Dad, siblings, or other family members in the household. Don't assume your child has better things to do than being with you. Make family dinners an expectation and you'll eventually see the positive changes that go along with this time spent together.

Carolina's story on pages 34 and 35 is not much different from the thousands of families struggling with homework issues at this very moment. Let's see how after-school life has changed since her parents have altered their approach.

Carolina-AFTER

It's 3 pm when Carolina arrives at home. She grabs a snack, chats with her friends over the phone and catches the end of her favorite soap opera. Just as she's agreed, Carolina opens her planner to determine what she must do for homework. At 3:30 she calls her mother, Marta, at work to let her know that she's home. She rattles off her assignments in the order in which she's going to complete them. By the time Marta gets home at 4:30, Carolina has most of her English finished. She's working in a new space in the spare bedroom that her parents use as a part-time office. She has a desk stocked with supplies just for her.

Marta commends her for excellent effort, especially the additional details she added to her research paper. At 5:00, Carolina gets ready for ballet. She returns at 7:00, has dinner with her family, and checks her planner once again.

Only math and social studies remain. The social studies work isn't actually an assignment; it's the first part of her upcoming project. Last week, Carolina and Marta did something they'd never done before – planned ahead for a long-term project. The problem, which had caused many arguments over the years, was discussed and solutions were agreed upon at their very first family meeting. That evening Carolina jotted down the incremental steps in her planner to keep on track for the final deadline.

By 8:30, Carolina is done with her work and she's even ahead of the game. Now her parents won't be breathing down her neck about the social studies project due next week! Marta quickly glances over Carolina's work, comparing it to the assignments listed in her notebook. Again, she congratulates her daughter for completing her work on time and for thinking ahead by working on the first step of her project. Carolina plops down on the sofa, cell phone in hand, having earned the privileges of screen time.

Carolina benefited from fair rules that she and her parents agreed upon. Not only were her parents pleased, but Carolina felt like she had control of the situation. She was no longer afraid that her parents were going to "snap" and yell at her one day, when they hadn't the day before. Life was much more predictable. There were days when Marta came home to find that homework hadn't even been contemplated because Carolina became absorbed in teenage life. But for the most part, the after-school hours were much easier. When the Juarez family felt that they were slipping back into their old ways, they would revisit the policies written in the family meeting book, and try to get back on track as quickly as possible. Carolina and her parents enjoyed the new normal.

Part II

Tips, Tools, And Solutions For Everyday Challenges And Concerns

How To Use This Book

In speaking to hundreds of parent groups on the topic of homework, I've found that mothers and fathers have only the best intentions of doing all the right things after school. They have a strong desire to help their children accept responsibility, work efficiently, and stay organized. Parents want to ensure that their kids are on top of their schoolwork and are reaching their potential. Universally, they yearn to raise children who are motivated to learn, succeed in school, and go out in the world to do good things.

If you are reading this book, you are one of these parents. However, somewhere along the way, there has been a glitch in the learning process for your child and homework has become more difficult than it needs to be. The first step to overcoming any homework stumbling block is to identify the homework profile or profiles of your child, and the second step is to explore your parenting habits. With these two answers in hand, you are on your way to taking much of the hassle out of homework.

If you've read the table of contents or flipped through this book, you've noticed that it contains solutions for the most common challenges. Whether your child is experiencing difficulty with: disorganization, rushing, procrastination, avoidance, distraction, frustration, or all of the above, you'll find the answers in the next few chapters. Solutions for all of these trouble spots are shared with you, the reader, through vignettes – real life situations to which you can relate.

The students I describe throughout this book vary in age, from elementary to high school. Although it may be appealing to look for quick answers by only reading the narratives of children in the same age bracket as your child, I encourage you to read each story and solution. Many of the strategies work just as well for a fifth grader as they do for a second or seventh grader, so don't be deterred by the ages of those profiled. Furthermore, you may find that the ideas I suggest for a student younger than yours are helpful as these solutions often involve building a strong foundation.

Start With Just A Few Strategies

This book contains almost 100 ideas for solving frequent, yet challenging, homework problems, but please don't feel overwhelmed. My goal is to present simple strategies to choose from as necessary. Pick a couple of easy-to-implement ideas that are feasible for both you and your child – ones that you can commit to on a consistent basis. It truly takes three weeks to establish a new pattern of behavior, but the time you invest will pay off down the road. I look forward to working with you to transform evenings fraught with frustration and disappointment to ones filled with harmony and success.

Chapter 4

What To Do About
The Disorganized

Goals

In this chapter you will learn how to help your child:

- Use checklists to stay organized.

- Create and maintain a binder system so that the correct papers get to and from school.

- Use techniques to keep an organized locker and/or desk.

- Set up a home study zone stocked with just the right materials.

- Archive old papers for future reference.

- Maintain newly found organizational skills through weekly check-ins.

The famous actor and director, Woody Allen, once said, "Eighty percent of success is showing up." I would amend that slightly: Eighty percent of school success is showing up AND staying organized. I've taught many students over the years who struggled fiercely in school. Those who were organized managed to stay afloat and achieve success. On the other hand, I've worked with tremendously gifted students for whom learning came easy, but their grades did not reflect their true abilities. They stumbled because their poor organizational skills impacted them in each and every subject area.

Does This Sound Familiar?

Test it Out!	A Usually	B Sometimes	C Rarely
My child can't find the materials needed to complete his homework.			
Important books and papers are left behind at school, leaving my child unprepared for homework.			
My child's backpack is filled with miscellaneous papers, many dated months ago.			
My child has difficulty staying on top of assignments, often turning work in late.			
His binder is messy with papers shoved into random places.			
My child seems to need more help staying organized than others his age.			
Long-term assignments, such as reports and projects, are done at the last minute.			
My child's grades would be better if he could be more organized.			
There have been times when my child actually completed the work, but could not locate it at school the next day.			
I have to remind my child to clear out his folders, binder, or backpack.			
The teacher tells me that my child is very bright, but also inconsistent and scattered.			

Total number of checks in each column	A	B	C

If you answered "usually" or "sometimes" to the majority of these questions, this chapter is for you. I encourage you to read on even if your student is exhibiting only some of these issues. Putting a basic organizational system in place is beneficial for all children.

What's Causing Such A Mess?

It is unlikely any child wakes up in the morning and decides he wants a barrage of negative feedback from his parents and teachers about his lack of organization. Life is easier for those who have these skills. Organization, or lack thereof, is based in executive functions which are innate neurological processes. Individuals with adequate executive function skills are able to plan ahead, organize, strategize, and manage time. They know which assignments are on the agenda after school and have the ability to prioritize. Instinctively, when a big task is at hand, such as a research paper, they approach it methodically, one step at a time.

Students with slowly developing executive function skills don't come by these abilities naturally. Contrary to popular belief, these students are not lazy or willfully disobedient, and their poor performance is not a matter of needing to simply try harder. Instead, these children need more support than the average kid in order to find success.

The Trickle Down Effect

Because organization is such a crucial part of academic achievement, it's easy to understand how students struggling in this one area may be impacted in each and every subject. For example, if a student with adequate organizational skills has difficulty with geometry, he can still do well in chemistry, English, history and all of his other subjects. But when a student is disorganized, he has, in essence, a disability in every subject. With age, organizational skills generally improve. That is a good thing because, as schoolwork becomes more complex with each year, these abilities become increasingly important. This chapter will provide you with the strategies to facilitate the development of organizational skills, whether you have a young child, tween, or teen. And, if staying organized has been difficult for you in the past, you'll pick up some pointers that will help your family as a whole.

Set The Stage For Organization

Before you begin to roll up your sleeves to clean out that backpack and binder, first, take the following steps:

Step 1

DISCUSS ORGANIZATION

SAY THIS: *"I know I've been on your case a lot about being more organized. You're getting older and I don't want to nag you. Let's get prepared for the new semester by setting up an organization system that works for you. Do you have some ideas?"*

OR THIS: *"I've been thinking about how we fight over homework – especially staying organized. I wish our evenings could be less stressful. What do you think is causing assignments and papers to be delayed or go missing? Can you think of a better way? I have a couple of ideas that may help. Let's start out the week on a good note by cleaning out your binder on Sunday evening after dinner."*

Step 2
SET UP A "TIME TO TALK"

With your child, agree on a specific day and time to start the process of getting more organized. Set aside 30-60 minutes. Think about scheduling this meeting at a time that would be most beneficial, such as:

- On Sunday, to prepare for the upcoming week and beyond.

- Before a new quarter, semester, or school year.

- On the first day of the month.

Step 3
BE NON-JUDGEMENTAL

Depending on your child's willingness, you may only have one shot at making this work. As tempting as it may be to say, "I've never seen such a mess!" when you unzip the backpack for the first time, hold back. There are many strategies in this chapter to help with organization, but they will not work if your child feels he is put on the defensive. Perhaps the most important ingredient to ensure success is your ability to remain non-non-judgmental.

 ### HELP IS ON THE WAY!
TOOLS FOR THE DISORGANIZED STUDENT

The Problem

Garrett - A Scattered Second Grader

Donna is a highly methodical, efficient, and driven mother who wants the best for her son, Garrett. She cannot understand how he can be so messy at such a young age. Garrett is warm and loving, with an infectious sense of humor. On the other hand, he is also lackadaisical and disorganized. He never seems to bring the right papers home and is always playing catch up with his assignments. Garrett is one of those kids who seems to leave a paper trail behind him wherever he goes.

Donna came to my office to discuss ways to help her son. I listened to her concerns, taking copious notes. She began by wringing her hands and sharing, "He's nothing like me. I don't know where he gets it. Last week he couldn't find a study guide for a test. When I insisted that he empty his backpack, he retrieved a moldy sandwich, crumpled papers, and a folder that he could barely pull out because it was stuck to the lining with gum. When I unfolded each crumpled paper, I eventually found the lost study guide."

It was hard for Donna to truly understand Garrett's struggles because organization came so easily to her. I was concerned because, after all, Garrett was only eight years old and had many years to go in school. We had to find a way to alleviate the source of contention.

The Solution

 ## Tip 1: Appreciate Differences

It was tough for Donna to understand that Garrett was a very different person from her. At times, she felt that if he cared about neatness or was just more motivated, the problem would go away. That was not the case; Garrett's difficulties were part of who he was. Although his executive functioning skills would progress as he got older, it is likely that organization will never be a strength for Garrett. Donna had functioned as an efficient, Type A go-getter for so many years that taking a step back and becoming more accepting of her son's differences was difficult for her. In time, Donna began to realize that criticizing her son got both of them nowhere. She needed to help him learn the right kind of strategies so that he could positively associate organization, homework, and learning.

 ## Tip 2: Create A Routine To Foster Organization And Put It In Writing

Donna and her other two children were naturally organized people, so she thought everyone else functioned the same way. She assumed that Garrett would be able to follow a basic after-school routine without losing materials, creating a mess in his homework area, or leaving important papers in random places. But he could not; he needed an external structure to compensate for his lack of the internal structure needed to get things done.

The fact was that he just couldn't do this alone, but he showed marked improvement once we created and posted a checklist. Prior to the checklist, he would throw his backpack in any old place, strew his papers across the kitchen table, and leave his completed work on the counter. No wonder he could not find his homework the next day at school. The checklist on the next page served as a visual reminder for Garrett. After a few months, he didn't need to refer to it each time he walked through the door. He started to remember the pattern and needed little prompting to follow through with the steps.

Organization  Checklist

Have I...

✓ Placed my backpack in the study area when coming home from school?

✓ Kept school papers in the study area?

✓ Put completed assignments into my homework folder?

✓ Put the homework folder into my backpack?

✓ Placed my backpack by the door?

 ## Tip 3: Establish A Homework Area

Donna found that setting up a special area, dedicated for homework and relatively free of distractions, helped Garrett. An elementary and middle school child should have one or two potential study areas that are clear of clutter, such as:

- The kitchen table.

- The dining room table (my favorite).

- A home office (on the main level – it's too hard to monitor homework time if it's occurring upstairs or in the basement).

High school (and responsible middle school) students can work in any of the above areas or in their rooms, as long as they have a table or desk. Some students may need access to a computer; however, they can be easily distracted by the internet. Just checking a few emails can turn into an hour of surfing the web and instant messaging with friends. If this has been a concern in the past, but your child genuinely needs computer access in order to type and print work, equip it with word processing software, not an internet connection. Research can be conducted on a computer in a common area that you are able to periodically monitor. If your child continues to waste time surfing the web, ask him to print out what he needs and then turn off the monitor to remove this distraction.

Of equal importance is having school supplies in one central location so that time is not wasted searching here, there, and everywhere for pens, pencils, or paper. Label a shoe box with the child's name or purchase a shower caddy to keep materials upright. This way, if the homework location must change for a night or two, supplies are portable. Each student will need supplies specific to his grade level, but the basics include:

- Lined paper

- Calculator

- Post-it notes

- Pencils and erasable pens

- Glue, scissors, and ruler

- Markers, highlighters, and colored pencils

- Electronic handheld spell checker (Franklin is a great brand)

 Tip 4: Create And Label A Dedicated Homework Folder

It's never too early to begin good organizational habits. From the day the very first assignment is given, a separate homework folder is necessary. Garrett already had such a folder, so I encouraged Donna to take it a step further and label one pocket "To Be Completed" and the other "Completed." This is important so that youngsters get in the habit very early on of putting schoolwork in the correct place. When an assignment is given in class, it should be placed in the left pocket and when it's finished at home, it goes in the right pocket. Repeat the mantra, "Homework isn't done until it's in your folder" until this process is automatic.

Tip 5: Give A Bonus For Staying Organized

Giving a bonus is a great way to incentivize any child. A bonus is a small reward that is above and beyond what the child is already earning for appropriate behavior. Garrett was expected to follow all the steps on his checklist described in Tip 2. His reward was free time to do whatever he pleased after 7 pm. If he followed the steps with only two reminders from Donna, then he could begin his free time at 6:45 pm.

A bonus can be given for almost any behavior you want to recognize and reward, and it doesn't have to be used in tandem with a checklist. For example, if you want your child to be packed up and ready for school before he goes to bed, and not at the last moment in the morning, give him a bonus for having all materials in his backpack by 8 pm. In terms of improving organization, consider a bonus for the following:

- Keeping a tidy binder (binder check can be daily, or just once per week).

- Putting completed work into the binder and placing it in the backpack.

- Keeping the study area neat by cleaning up after homework.

A bonus can be anything that is of value to the child, such as:

- Additional computer time.

- A special dessert after dinner.

- A later bedtime.

- A small amount of money in addition to his allowance.

Bonuses don't have to be given daily. In fact, an unexpected bonus is sometimes more meaningful and motivating than expected rewards. I've found that kids are likely to change their disorganized habits when they're supported with the right strategies and incentives. This is a far better approach than punishment or constant verbal reprimands.

The Problem

Kwon – A Muddled Middle School Student

Kwon wasn't alone in his cluttered world. His parents had a hard time staying organized, too. I knew I could help Kwon turn things around so that his grades wouldn't suffer due to his disorganization, but I had my work cut out for me with his parents. Upon arriving at their home for my initial visit, it was clear that there were no specified areas for completing homework, keeping track of school papers, or the kids' schedules. The three children's backpacks were strewn randomly – one in the hallway, one on the kitchen counter, and the other on the kitchen floor. The dining room table served as the kids' homework area, but it was piled high with magazines and old mail.

Problem cont.

Kwon's teacher, Mrs. Green, reported that he was not completing his homework, but his mother, Sue, stated that it did indeed get done each night. And of course, Kwon vouched for that fact. In addition, Mrs. Green said that Kwon's desk was a real mess. He was never ready to switch classes because he had such trouble finding the right books, folders, and pencils. She said that his messy habits spilled over to the floor as there were papers scattered within a three foot radius.

In order to assist Kwon, I had to develop routines and systems within his household as well. Truly, his family needed a professional organizer to tackle the whole house, but I focused on organizational systems that were needed for academic success.

The Solution

 Tip 1: Use "The Study Zone"

As a 6th grader, Kwon wasn't ready to do homework in his bedroom because he still needed some parental oversight. The dining room table was the perfect spot, but we had to clear half of it off in order to make it usable. Kwon needed a portable work station – enter The Study Zone. The Study Zone, developed by educational consultant, Ilene Schwartz (www.strategiceducationalsolutions.com) provides an enclosed work space and accessible organizers for supplies and important papers. This concept was perfect for Kwon because when he opened and expanded The Study Zone, it became his own little homework island. The panels blocked out household distractions, and he was less likely to misplace supplies because there was a place for everything. More importantly, it didn't take up much space and could be easily moved.

Weekly schedule

Subject folders

Archived Papers

Post-it notes Erasers

Pens Pencils High-lighters

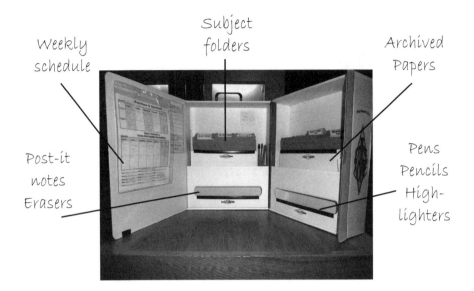

 Tip 2: Create A Launching Pad

A Launching Pad is a contained space for everything related to school that needs to get out the door each morning. In essence, it launches the child into the day, equipped with all the right essentials – backpack, lunch box, library books, etc. A Launching Pad can be a box, large basket, dishpan, or any container big enough to house your child's school items. Put it in a well traveled area, preferably near the door your child enters and exits from each school day. Since the dining room was adjacent to the garage door entrance, and it was home to his Study Zone, we placed a beige, fabric container on the table and used the back of the dining room chair to hang his coat. Now, all school materials were in one place for Kwon. In fact, his siblings liked this approach so much, that Kwon's mother cleared off the rest of the dining room table to make room for the other children.

Backpack

Other school materials

Lunch

Launching Pad

Once we set up the Launching Pad, Kwon had a system in place that helped maintain organization. When he came home from school, he tossed his backpack and school books into the Launching Pad. All school-related items were expected to stay in the same area. His parents got into the act, too. If they found a stray school paper, they put it in the bin. Permission slips and weekly folders that needed to be signed by a parent were placed there as well. Now, there was much less school-related clutter around the home.

Tip 3: Create The Simple Solution

Over the years, I've seen many kids struggle to keep up with a binder system that just doesn't work for them. Kwon was a prime example. He used a binder that contained an elaborate filing system which required constant upkeep. Even though it contained tabs, folders, and pockets, Kwon never used any of them. Instead, he layered all of his papers on top of each other and placed them in a stack next to the rings – not in the rings, but next to them. If he didn't hold the binder from the bottom, all the loose papers fell out.

Kwon admitted that he hated to hole punch and file using the traditional three-ring system. This didn't at all surprise me because many disorganized students feel the same way. Kwon needed a different solution, one that was easy to use and maintain. I introduced him to a system I have created for many of my students. I call it, "The Simple Solution." It's easy to create and just may work for your child, too.

Step 1: The first step is to purchase a binder containing an accordion folder. The pull out accordion folder is where all papers are filed. This way, there's no hole punching involved. The one I often use is made by Case It (www.caseit.com).

Step 2: Label each section tab with the subject name (Math, Science, English, etc.). File all papers behind the correct subject tab, putting the most recent pages toward the back. This ensures they are in chronological order. Papers can accumulate quickly, so it's important to archive old materials routinely. Check out pages 76-77 for an easy archiving system.

Step 3: Your child will use the small three-ring section for multiple purposes, but his first and foremost priority should be his planner, which must always be secured in the front. It should not be removed from the binder unless absolutely necessary as loose planners have a tendency to get lost.

Step 4: Behind the planner, secure a pocket folder anchored into the three rings. This is a dedicated folder for homework in all subjects. The left pocket should be labeled "To Be Completed" and the right pocket "Completed." Assignments given by teachers are always placed on the left and once they're done, they're moved to the right. This method is far superior to randomly putting homework in the backpack, tucking it into a book or another miscellaneous folder. Now, there's no doubt where the completed work is located.

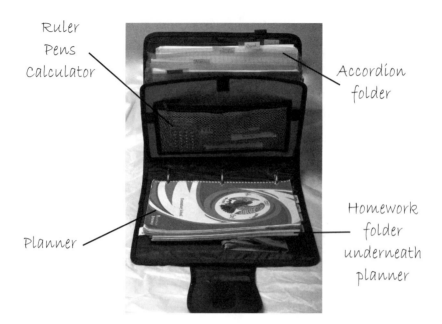

Ruler
Pens
Calculator

Accordion folder

Planner

Homework folder underneath planner

Based on class schedule and subjects, as well as teachers who require different types of notebooks, you may want to have a two-binder system.

One binder for:	The other for:
Classes before lunch	Classes after lunch
Math/Science related classes	English/History related classes
Block scheduling A days	Block scheduling B days
Core classes	Non-core classes

Step 5: Lastly, papers that need to be referenced regularly can be inserted into plastic page protectors and secured behind the homework folder. These pages will vary based on the child's age, but may include the student's class schedule or frequently used information, such as a periodic table or multiplication chart. This section is not always necessary, but is an option if your child will use it.

Tip 4: Ensure That The Right Materials Come Home

At the end of the school day, the last thing kids want to think about is homework. Bringing the correct books, folders, and papers home is a common problem that impacts many students, even the most organized. For Kwon, this is where the breakdown occurred. What was needed for homework didn't always make its way out of his desk.

I suggested that he keep a plastic bin at the foot of his desk. As soon as he received a homework assignment, he was to put all related books into the bin. This was easy when he was at his homeroom desk, but more of a challenge when he switched classes because the bin wasn't readily available. Kwon improvised by placing all homework on top of the stack of books he carried back to his homeroom class. The minute he returned, those materials went straight into the bin. The end of the day was much less hectic now for Kwon because he simply had to dump everything from the container into his backpack.

Although this didn't make for a tidy backpack, he was able to achieve the goal of bringing home the right materials. When there was time, Kwon was able to neatly file homework "to do" papers into his homework folder. However, when he felt rushed, I told him that it was okay, to place everything in the bin.

Tip 5: Declutter The Desk

Kwon and his family had come a long way. He now had a special place for homework, a Launching Pad, and a solution for transporting the right supplies to and from school. There was one nagging problem in the back of my mind. Kwon's teacher mentioned weeks before that his desk was very disorganized, so I decided to meet with Kwon one day at school after his classes were over to see if I could be of assistance. It was no surprise that he needed help at school, too. There were crumpled papers crammed into his desk, loose papers everywhere, and about 15 pencils that he really didn't need. Kwon and I discussed how he'd like to organize his desk, and we came up with the idea to place hardcover texts on the left, and paperback books, spiral notebooks, and folders on the right. His writing utensils went into a pouch.

A teacher friend once said to me – "You know a child's desk is disorganized when you put your fist through the middle and don't touch metal on the backside." It's true. If your hand only hits unfastened papers, then the desk needs straightening. Kwon liked this little test to determine for himself if he needed to perform a clean out. If your child is willing, stop by his classroom before or after school to help him declutter his desk.

No Organization System

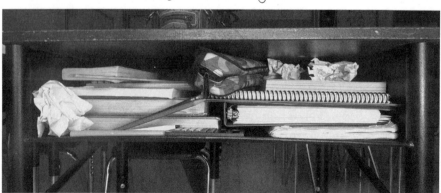

Hardcover texts

Large items at the bottom of each pile

Binder, folders and soft covered books

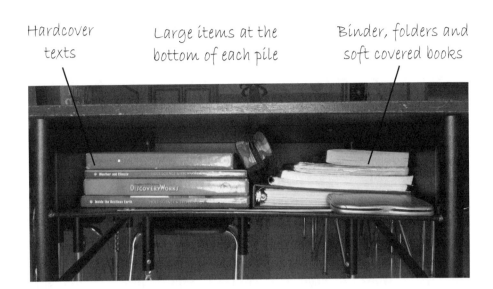

The Problem

Candice – A Ninth Grader Struggling To Stay Organized In High School

Candice was diagnosed with ADHD as a fifth grader. Her teacher commented that she was well behaved and "a joy to have in class," but that she seemed "spacey." Candice flew under her teacher's radar screen in the primary grades because she was able to keep up in class and never caused any trouble. By her fifth grade year, problems with organization started to become apparent. Gone were the days she could rifle through her own desk for papers, books, and pencils. Now, she had to remember to bring the right materials from class to class. She was never ready when called upon by her teacher.

Presently in ninth grade, she is totally unprepared to keep an organized locker, maintain her binder, and stay on top of seven teachers'

Problem cont.

expectations. She's always backpedaling – turning in assignments late, asking for extensions, and borrowing her friends' books when she can't find hers. Candice is becoming increasingly anxious and fearful. She said, "It seems like I can never get caught up. Even when I do, there's another project right around the corner. I hate this constant ache in the pit in my stomach."

As I began to assist Candice's family, her parents asked the same question many others do. "Where should we begin? Our daughter is scattered in every facet of her life." Because Candice's disorganization was impacting her the most in school, I suggested that we first tackle her binder system. The binder is the student's lifeline to school and home. Without a well-maintained binder, academic success is virtually impossible as the right papers won't make it home and even completed homework will never find its way back to the teacher's in-box. The steps to an organized binder described here are one solution, however, your child may have a different idea in mind. The goal is to have a system in place that can be easily maintained. Allow choice, because what works for one student may not be right for another.

The Solution

 ### Tip 1: Use One System

Candice kept a one inch, three-ring binder for each of her seven classes. It was clear that keeping track of all seven was too much for her, but she was adamant about keeping them separate. When I suggested one

74

larger binder, she resisted. For some reason, she just couldn't give up the way she'd always done things, even though it clearly wasn't working for her. I continued to push. Eventually we reached a happy medium. She kept all of her small binders, but agreed to utilize a uniform system for each one.

You can help your child create individual binder systems, by securing two folders with two pockets each in a binder. One folder is for homework; its pockets should be labeled "to be completed" and "completed." The other folder should have one pocket for either a composition book, spiral notebook or looseleaf notes and be labeled "notes". The other pocket should be labeled "handouts and returned papers."

Two Things A Binder Should Include:
1. Homework Folder in Front with Two Pockets
One labeled "To be completed"
Other labeled "Completed"
2. Second Folder with Two Pockets
One labeled "For Notes"
One labeled "For Handouts"

Instead of separate binders or spiral notebooks, some students prefer using an expandable accordion folder. In lieu of labeling pocket folders as explained above, simply label the accordion folder's tabs in the same manner.

A uniform system should be set up for each core class binder. Your child may wish to use this labeling system or one of her own, but the main idea is to find a consistent way to keep track of materials. When one system is used for multiple subjects, the student is more likely to feel at ease with keeping papers in the right place.

Tip 2: Set Up A System For Archiving Papers

Papers inside of any kind of binder system can pile up quickly. Students keep months' worth of work without clearing old materials out or they take the opposite approach and purge everything. A useful compromise is to use a file box to archive important papers on a regular basis. As students get older, cumulative exams, mid-terms, and finals containing test material from earlier in the year or quarter become the norm. Such exams are one of the Disorganized student's worst nightmares because they cannot find previously completed work from which to study. You can help your child overcome this obstacle.

- At the end of each quarter or month, have your child remove papers not related to the current unit of study.

- Label each section in the file box with a subject name.

- Prompt your child to file papers behind the appropriate subject tab. For papers related to a particular unit or chapter, paperclip them together with a cover sheet identifying the topic.

- Keep the archiving system at home so that papers don't get lost.

- Post reminders on the family calendar or program the reminder into your phone and have your child do the same. This will ensure that archiving is done regularly.

This archiving system should stay on top of your child's desk or study area, so the information is easily accessible. If it goes into a drawer, it will be forgotten.

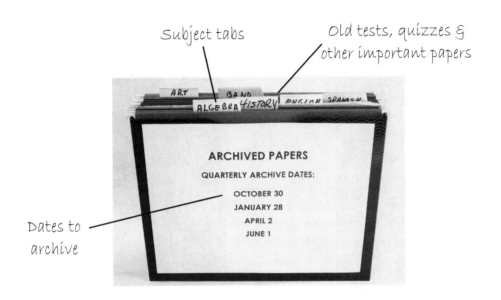

Subject tabs

Old tests, quizzes & other important papers

Dates to archive

ARCHIVED PAPERS

QUARTERLY ARCHIVE DATES:

OCTOBER 30
JANUARY 28
APRIL 2
JUNE 1

 ## Tip 3: Organize The Locker

Some schools require students to use their lockers daily as they aren't allowed to carry backpacks from class to class. This was the case with Candice; therefore, an organized locker was an important part of school success. Candice asked me for help with her locker, so I met her after school one afternoon and we got to work.

In the following pictures, you can see how Candice's locker looked before and then after we met. The key with Candice, and all students, is to set up a system that is easy to use and maintain. We organized her locker by block schedules – red days and black days; however, the system can vary based on the student's need.

Because Candice's locker didn't have enough shelves, we used Locker Works' three-tiered, hanging shelving unit (www.locker-works.com). This system can hold heavy books, but is flexible for larger items, such as backpacks and coats.

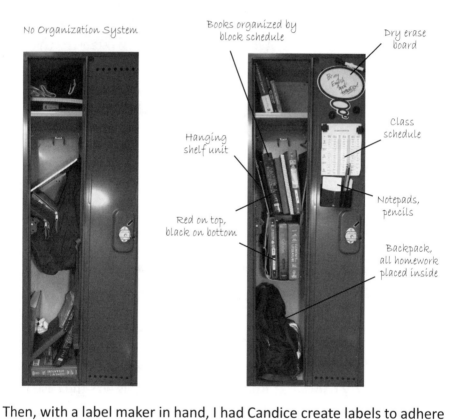

Then, with a label maker in hand, I had Candice create labels to adhere to each shelf or section. Lastly, she hung a dry erase board inside the locker door so that she could easily jot down any important notes.

If you have a sneaking suspicion that your child's locker could be in disarray, open a dialogue. Your child may not want you to pay a visit to school, but you can at least find out what she needs, visit a local supply store, and let her pick out necessities such as those outlined above. Encourage your child to stay after school or arrive early one morning to get reorganized.

Another approach is to do the work at home by equipping her with shopping bags to retrieve all materials from her locker. Arrange to pick her up from school and upon returning home, have her sort and purge, determining what can stay at home and what needs to return to school. Place all of these items into a bag along with any newly purchased shelving units so that she can reorganize her locker before school the following morning. Clearing out a locker is best done at naturally occurring breaks such as the beginning of a new quarter, first of the month, or just before or after a holiday break, giving the student a fresh start.

 ## Tip 4: Schedule a Clean Sweep

Anyone can create an organizing system, but the real test is maintaining it. Whether you want to help your child keep his binder, backpack, homework area, or Launching Pad organized, you need to schedule regular maintenance sessions. Candice's, Kwon's, and Garrett's parents were amazed to find that having a pre-arranged weekly maintenance session, called Clean Sweep, kept their kids on top of organization.

In your family, you can easily remember these half hour sessions a couple of ways. One option is to purchase a large monthly desk calendar at your local office supply store. Alternatively, take a look at the website www.MomAgenda.com for a magnetic weekly family planner that will hold your schedule and up to four children's after-school activities as well. Either option will serve as your family calendar is so that everyone knows when this maintenance meeting occurs. Many families find that Sunday evening is an ideal time to prepare for the week ahead. When this is clearly written on the calendar, you'll have less resistance as it becomes part of the family routine.

Another way to keep abreast of your maintenance meeting is to program the set time, say Sunday from 7 to 7:30 pm into your Blackberry, iPhone, or other device. Have your children do the same if they own a cell phone. Activate the alarm so that you receive a 15-minute warning that your maintenance meeting is just around the corner. During this maintenance session, your children will be responsible for organizing anything related to school. Don't assume when you say, "We're going to spend the next half hour organizing," they will know what to do. Create and post a checklist of what needs to be accomplished. Your children's checklist might look like this:

Weekly Clean Sweep

- ✓ Organize your binder.
- ✓ Clean out your backpack.
- ✓ Restock school supplies (those at home and for school).
- ✓ Clear off your study area.
- ✓ Tidy the Launching Pad.

This is also a great time to model the skills you're teaching. Update the family calendar, sort through mail, or organize your work space. Make sure you're available to assist if necessary. Candice's parents found that the Clean Sweep also provided an an opportunity for them to check in with their daughter about long-term assignments. They discussed the progress being made with projects, reports, and other large tasks.

As time goes on, your kids will require less work and time to sustain neatness, but don't stop this routine. Try meeting every other week if your child now has the tools to stay organized independently.

Chapter 4
Homework Made Simple
Checklist

You can support and maintain organization for your child by utilizing fundamental strategies. Have you:

- ✓ Set up and stocked a dedicated homework area?

- ✓ Crafted a Launching Pad?

- ✓ Helped your child find and use a specific binder system?

- ✓ Created an archiving bin to save important papers?

- ✓ Assisted with desk or locker organization?

- ✓ Instituted a weekly Clean Sweep session?

Chapter 5

What To Do About The Rusher

Goals

In this chapter you will learn to help your Rusher by:

- Discussing expectations BEFORE homework begins.

- Setting up Dedicated Homework Time.

- Parenting proactively instead of reactively.

- Allowing your child to get her work done independently.

- Setting high, but realistic expectations.

"My kid always rushes through her homework!" I hear this complaint from many parents. As adults, it's difficult for us to understand why our children can't slow down, take time to focus, and check their work.

Rushing is not a serious issue if your child occasionally races through homework because she has "better things to do." Rushing only becomes a problem when your child can't slow down, seems unmotivated to do well, and often turns in work that is inaccurate and contains careless errors. For this type of student, rushing is frequently a daily habit.

The positive aspect of rushing is that these kids usually get their work done. Although it may not be up to their parents' or teachers' expectations, at least they aren't taking hours to complete assignments. I've found that when these students start to internalize self-regulation strategies and are rewarded for even minor attention to detail, work quality improves.

Does This Sound Familiar?

Test It Out!	A Usually	B Sometimes	C Rarely
My child completes homework quickly, with little attention to detail.			
My child's grades suffer because of careless mistakes.			
I argue with my child over the quality of homework.			
My child does homework so quickly that her handwriting is messy or illegible.			
My child isn't motivated to do her best work, just to get it done.			
The teacher says that my child is capable of a higher quality of work, if only she would take the time.			
I notice that my child spends little time on any activity she doesn't find exciting. Even chores and personal care are done hurriedly.			
My child avoids editing, proofreading, and/or revising written work.			

Total number of checks in each column	A	B	C

If you answered "usually" or "sometimes" to most of these questions, this chapter's for you.

Why Students Rush

The first step in helping students who rush is to uncover the reason why they are doing so. Take a step back and observe your child doing homework. Then ask these questions:

- Is she merely working too quickly so that she can move on to a more enjoyable activity?

- Are his tendencies to rush in particular subjects really signals that the work has become too laborious or difficult?

- Is the work too easy? Could she be bored?

- Does he feel that he is overscheduled and has little room for downtime?

The Need For Immediate Gratification

Sometimes, the reason for rushing may not be obvious. There are many students who simply need immediate gratification. By completing a task, they are providing their brain with the quick fix of accomplishment. They have difficulty delaying gratification, so they work quickly to gain the feeling of having the assignment done and off their plate. Working methodically is especially tough for these students and no matter how many times they're reminded to "slow down" they continue to to race ahead.

When It's More Than Just
The Desire To Play

There are instances when rushing through homework is a coping mechanism for avoiding what is too difficult or frustrating. In my experience, the most pronounced areas of struggle for these kids are writing and math. Their writing may be simplistic even when verbal abilities are excellent. So often Rushers will write the bare minimum just to earn an acceptable grade. This was the case with Ethan, whom you'll read about on the following pages. As I began to tutor Ethan on a one-to-one basis, it became apparent that he lacked many of the underlying skills necessary to write on grade level.

There is a difference, however, between the Rusher and a student who truly struggles with written language. Some children may have learning issues that manifest themselves as difficulties with spelling, poor handwriting, and trouble putting thoughts on paper. Before assuming that your child just doesn't want to put forth adequate effort, be sure that there aren't other underlying problems. Talk to your child's teacher or consult a learning disabilities specialist if you feel that there may be more than meets the eye. The children I'm referring to in this chapter can produce excellent work with little intervention when they work for a longer period of time and are given cues for checking their work.

Math And Rushing Do NOT Mix!

Math is another subject area that creates stumbling blocks for the Rusher. Often times these students understand the concepts, but work too hastily. Failure to focus on details such as computational signs or negative and positive numbers can lead to incorrect answers. In addition, Rushers tend to avoid showing their work because they think they can hold answers to intermediate steps in their head. This often is not the case, especially when the problems become more complicated.

Keep in mind that despite the pros and cons of this behavior, not all rushing is such a bad thing. When grades are good and your child is happy and successful in the classroom, intervention may not be necessary. If this is the case with your youngster, choose just one or two simple strategies from this chapter.

HELP IS ON THE WAY!
TOOLS FOR THE RUSHER

The Problem

Ethan – A 4th Grader Who Rushes To Finish

Ethan was a freckled-faced fourth grader who was in daily battles with his mother about homework, even at such a young age. His mother, Vera, contacted me because she realized that there was no way she was going to make it through the remainder of Ethan's school career without a breakdown. Vera was an excellent student as a child and couldn't quite understand why Ethan didn't share her zest for learning.

Once Ethan settled down to homework, he worked too quickly. He almost always forgot to label his papers correctly (name, date, and page number) and typically answered questions incorrectly because he did not read the directions carefully. Vera was tired of constantly questioning him with, "Did you write your name on your paper?" or "Can you put more effort into this?" His habit of rushing was causing undue stress in the parent/child relationship.

The Solution

Tip 1: Set Expectations BEFORE Homework Begins

Rushers do best when parents state their expectations up-front. I suggested that Vera let Ethan know her expectations before he started his homework, not after he finished his work. Although Vera wanted to change many of Ethan's careless tendencies, I encouraged her to start with just one or two. She identified the tasks that he typically rushed through and, instead of constant verbal reminders, she simply jotted one or two visual reminders on a Post-it note. This can work for your child, too. Jot down one to three bullet points on a Post-it note and place near the assignment.

Expectations will vary based on the age of the student and the subject, but examples may include:

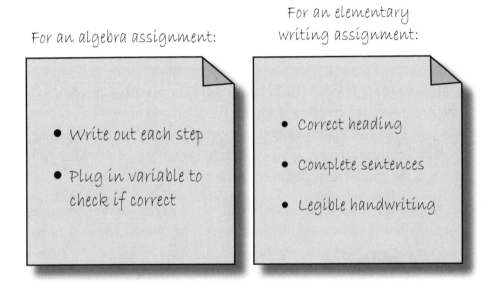

For an algebra assignment:

- Write out each step

- Plug in variable to check if correct

For an elementary writing assignment:

- Correct heading

- Complete sentences

- Legible handwriting

Be sure to target just a few action items. Setting the bar too high can turn off your child to learning.

 Tip 2: Chunk Time For Best Results

Paying attention to detail is truly difficult for many students. Often, it's unrealistic to expect young children to work slowly and methodically for an extended period of time, but they can do it in spurts. Vera wanted Ethan to work slowly in math, writing down each step neatly and checking each problem. This wasn't realistic; he just couldn't sustain that level of focus for the entire homework assignment. Knowing that Ethan could work in short bursts, I encouraged her to say, "Do the first five problems the best you can, then you may do the rest quickly." Of course, he loved this idea. Slowly, he was able to stretch the number of problems he could do to six, seven, and later on, eight. The goal was to increase the length of time he was able to sustain attention to detail.

I also encouraged Vera to set a timer for a short period of time and to choose an odd number like 6 or 11 minutes – that's more interesting than 5 or 10. She said to her son, "Work as slowly and as carefully as you can during this time." Again, she gradually increased the amount of time as he demonstrated that he was consistently able to meet this goal. Timers are effective tools for Rushers because they're neutral. A timer removes the emotion from the situation and means parents are less prone to questioning or constantly checking in. In the beginning, the adult controls the timer. As your child becomes more familiar with this tool, he can be responsible for setting it.

After a few days, Ethan's work was far neater and more accurate, but Vera felt it still wasn't his best work. At times, only part of his assignment was neat (usually the section done while using the timer) Although this was true, the bottom line was that he made significant improvements, and that alone was reason to celebrate. I asked her not to correct each and every problem or criticize the work that was a bit sloppy. As the weeks passed, Ethan started to internalize the slow and steady pace. He got into the habit of working more carefully; his overall work quality improved.

 ## Tip 3: Use P-N-P For Praise

Perhaps the most important tip for helping a Rusher is to recognize any sign of good work, no matter how small it may be. In the past, Vera was quick to notice Ethan's mistakes. She used Tip 1 - jotting down one or two visual reminders on a Post-it note before Ethan started his homework, and she saw that change was occurring. One day, I was observing a homework session in Vera's home. Although she had followed my instructions for Tips 1 and 2, it was clear that the missing element was praise. When I asked her why she didn't praise Ethan when he finally wrote the assignment title (Math pg. 26) and dated his paper, she replied, "Well, he should do that anyway." She was right; Ethan should have completed this basic step on his own. But the plain fact was that he never remembered to do it in the past independently.

I coached her to always notice positive changes, even if they are very minor. It was Vera's unconscious nature to acknowledge Ethan's failures before ever saying anything positive. We worked on always starting with a positive statement first, using the "P-N-P Sandwich" approach, or Positive-Negative-Positive. Begin with a positive statement, follow with constructive criticism, and end with another positive comment.

Positive	Negative	Positive
"I like the way you wrote these sentences so neatly!"	*"The answer to #3 needs a few more details."*	*"I can see you worked hard to use a lot of vivid adjectives!"*
"Outstanding effort finding the vocabulary words in the glossary!"	*"I noticed that the definition for 'bare' is incorrect."*	*"I'm happy to see that you wrote detailed definitions!"*

Constructive feedback should contain specific, concrete suggestions. If an adult's comments are too vague, the child may become frustrated because he doesn't explicitly know what he needs to change. So, instead of "You can do better than this!" try saying, "You only need to fix problem number two."

The Problem

Gianna - A 6th Grader Who Would NOT Slow Down

Gianna was one of those highly verbal kids who never seemed to stop moving. She was engaging, bright, and full of energy. Gianna's parents, Maria and Salvador, were divorced with shared custody; Gianna split the weekdays between households. Although her parents were generally in agreement about homework, they struggled daily to help Gianna curb her habit of rushing. Both of her parents reported that she would do the least amount of work necessary to get by. Before they turned around, she was out the door, hanging out with the kids in the neighborhood. When there was no one in sight, Gianna was quick to jump on the computer and begin instant messaging with her friends.

I worked with both parents and Gianna over a school year. I first recommended that they implement the strategies shared with you in Ethan's story (Post-it notes for expectations, use of the timer, and praise). Although these strategies helped, Maria and Salvador found that Gianna was increasingly reluctant to listen to them. In addition, Salvador felt like he was at a loss for what to do when Gianna reported that she had no homework or that she had completed it in school. On days Gianna stayed with him, she miraculously never had homework.

Gianna's grades were not stellar; she was earning mostly C's. The teacher comments on her math papers were, "Please show your work," or "I can't read this." In language arts, the teacher comments included "Elaborate please," and "You can describe this in greater detail." It became clear that Maria and Salvador needed to have the exact same guidelines for their daughter.

The Solution

Tip 1: Establish A Dedicated Homework Time

I'm a big proponent of establishing a Dedicated Homework Time, otherwise known as DHT. It's a scheduled block of time each weekday that is dedicated to homework, whether the student says she has it or not. DHT helps break the rushing habit. Regardless of how quickly your child finishes homework, the entire DHT should be dedicated to academically related tasks. If she finishes before the DHT is up, she can study for a test, work on a long-term project, organize her notebook, or read. The general rule of thumb is that the total time spent doing homework be equivalent to 10 minutes per grade level.

Here's A Guide:	
Grade 1	10 minutes
Grade 2	20 minutes
Grade 3	30 minutes
Grade 4	40 minutes
Grades 5 and 6	50 or 60 minutes
Grades 7-12	1 hour (90 minutes is acceptable for high school students)

In Gianna's case, I recommended that a full 60 minutes be carved out of her schedule for DHT. Salvador and Maria agreed. Together we created a weekly schedule based on their custody arrangement and Gianna's extracurricular activities. Although she didn't begin her homework at the same time each day (this was impossible due to their busy lives), they each found 60 minutes daily, free of interruptions. In addition, they agreed not to allow access to any electronics during this time.

When DHT was first implemented, Gianna complained that the new policy wasn't fair. After a few weeks, she began to accept it. Interestingly, Salvador reported that Gianna went from never having homework (according to her) to actually having homework. Did her teachers suddenly begin doling out the work? No, it was that the family's expectations had changed. Gianna realized that if DHT wasn't going away she might as well find homework to do.

I've found that for many parents struggling with the homework issue, implementing DHT is the best place to start. The question then becomes, "How do I do it?"

Getting Started

To establish a Designated Homework Time, sit down with your child and discuss why you're implementing this new concept. It's best to have this discussion either at the beginning of a month, a new school week, or a new grading period. At this time, you may say, "I know homework has become stressful for both of us. Let's try this for the next month," or "Let's start this quarter off on a positive note." You can also talk about setting up a DHT after an argument has occurred, but only when everyone has calmed down (usually later that evening or the following day). Typically, both parent and child realize that something has to change at this point.

Tip 2: Create A DHT Menu

A common question regarding DHT is "What do you do if there's no homework assigned?" It's been my experience that there is almost always something to do. Ask your child to do a binder check. She'll probably find assignments she forgot about or is putting off. If there is really no homework, consider the following options:

Younger Children Can:

- Begin to work on an upcoming book report or project.

- Learn to keyboard if handwriting is consistently difficult to read. Keyboarding may be a better option. Try *Type to Learn* software to teach or improve typing skills.

- Drill math facts on an educational website or computer software. Some great websites are www.funbrain.com and www.multiplication.com.

- Simply read a required book or choose one for pleasure.

Older Students Can:

- Plan ahead. Use this time to record all of his long-term projects along with incremental due dates.

- Work on anything that's not due the next day. All incremental deadlines have associated work. Getting ahead during the DHT is one of the best uses of time.

- Study for an upcoming test. Review old tests and quizzes or create a study guide similar to what may be on the test.

DHT worked wonders for Gianna's situation. She and her parents no longer argued about the minimal amount of time she spent on homework. In fact, Gianna's grades improved because she was turning in better quality homework.

However, Salvador and Maria did encounter one common problem. On some days, Gianna did not have much homework. When this occurred, they felt like they were constantly repeating the same ideas over and over. So, with Gianna, they created and posted a DHT menu on the family bulletin board. It contained a list of activities available to Gianna when she had no homework left to do.

Gianna's DHT MENU
File papers correctly in the binder.
Clean out the backpack and/or launching pad.
Record long-term assignments in planner.
Cuddle up with a book.
Work on monthly book report.

 Tip 3: Spot-Check Only!

Checking every single answer after your child completes his homework creates tension. The message you communicate is that your child isn't capable of success without you. Limiting your review to a spot check enables independence and also communicates the message that you care about effort. Instead of reviewing each answer, consider only checking the work you've targeted with Post-it notes, along with perhaps one other assignment for completion and accuracy.

If you have a middle or high school age student who you think would benefit from closer monitoring, make this process gradual, especially if you haven't been involved in the past. Introduce the idea by saying that you want to be more up-to-date on homework. If you observe your adolescent rushing through the work from a particular class, start there. Ask to see the homework assignment for that class. Tell him that you just want to glance over the completed assignment. The fact is you may not have any clue how to actually do the work. When was the last time you researched the Battle of the Bulge or balanced a chemical equation? When this is the case, just check for completeness.

In Gianna's family, this method, along with DHT, helped her to complete her work independently. When her 60 minutes of DHT was up, one of her parents asked to see her completed work. They did not check every answer but they made sure the work was done.

The Problem

Natasha – A 4th Grader Who Struggles With Writing And Following Directions

Last year, I had the privilege of working with an engaging girl, Natasha, and her mother, Malia. With her big smile, sparkling eyes, and warm personality, Natasha lit up a room. Although she was more than willing to work hard for me, homework with her mother's oversight was a different story.

Natasha and her mom were frequently engaged in arguments about following directions. Natasha would inadvertently read instructions for assignments incorrectly, and the end result would be an assignment that had to be redone. That wasn't the only problem. Malia felt that Natasha rushed through her writing which resulted in final products that were marred by incorrect grammar, poor spelling, and limited punctuation. Malia wanted a better way to help her daughter slow down, read directions, and check her written work. She wanted to assist Natasha in checking her written work so that it was a better reflection of her true abilities.

The Solution

 ## Tip 1: Use Color To Improve Attention To Directions

Because following directions was such a struggle for Natasha, I decided to use good old-fashioned highlighting to help her focus on important information. In our first session together, Natasha showed me what she had for homework that evening. One of the assignments was a workbook page. I asked her how she would get started. She replied, "That's easy! You do it like this." Natasha started on the first item without stopping to read the directions. So, I asked her to pick her favorite color highlighter and modeled for her and Malia how to highlight the key words in the directions. This simple trick worked wonders for Natasha and she agreed to use this approach from then on.

The use of color has been well researched. Dr. Sydney Zentall, a professor at Purdue University, has found that color is a powerful tool for helping students focus, improve accuracy, and work methodically. You can use color with your child in many ways, such as:

- After reading a passage or paragraph, coach your child to stop and reflect back on what he's read, and then have him highlight just the main points. Kids often make the mistake of highlighting as they read, so that by the end of the page, practically every line is marked. This "highlighter happy" approach does not work. Read first, pause and reflect, and then highlight.

- Use removable highlighting tape if the textbook is school property. I've found that kids enjoy this process and the best part is that when they need to review the chapter to study for a test, the main points are already marked. Then their review will consist of reading (and reciting if you can get them to do it) the highlighted sentences and removing the tape. You can purchase this product at www.reallygoodstuff.com.

- Highlight operational symbols in math with different colors. For example, use red for all subtraction signs and green for addition.

- Color can also help reading comprehension. In her book, *ADHD and Education*, Dr. Zentall states that when students used color as a reading guide, they improved their comprehension. You can do this with your child by encouraging her to use a brightly colored index card or a folded piece of colored paper. In order to make this strategy effective, start using the reading guide to track the lines at about the halfway point of the page. If it's used for the entire page, the color loses its novelty and effectiveness.

 ## Tip 2: Use The Right Words To Help With Writing

Malia found that she was greeted with a blank stare when she asked her daughter to edit and proofread her writing. Asking a child to correct each mistake is just like asking her to clean her room when it's so messy she can't even see the carpet. She has no idea where to start. When parents and teachers make this blanket request, they usually get one of two things – total resistance to starting or an end product peppered with mistakes.

While assisting with the final writing product, keep in mind that the more specific you are, the easier the task will seem for your child. Take a look at how parents of younger and older writers handle these situations.

Grade K-5 Situation	Instead of Saying This	Try Saying This
Your third grader did not take the time to correct his spelling mistakes.	"I see tons of mis-spelled words. Please fix them."	"I see eight errors. See how many you can find. Try using your Franklin Speller!"
Each week, your stepson must create 10 sentences from his spelling list. As in past weeks, his sentences are a meager 4 or 5 words long.	"You could do better work if only you slowed down. Try to add some more details to these sentences."	"Let's do the first sentence together so you get the hang of it." Watch him do the next one so you know he understands. Let him work alone.
Both of your children write so quickly, their work is barely legible. This time, you make an effort to address the issue BEFORE they begin.	"There is no way you're turning this mess in to your teacher! You have to rewrite it."	"You wrote the title neatly. If your sentences were within the margin lines, the paper would look orderly. Please make those changes."

Middle/ High School Situation	Instead of Saying This	Try Saying This
Writing has always been arduous for your high school sophomore. Lately you notice that he's revising his work more than usual.	"It's about time! I'm so glad you're finally putting in some effort after all these years!"	"The extra time you're spending is really paying off. I can see a difference in the way you are using details to express your thoughts."
Your daughter is working on paragraph development, but you see that her sentences don't flow together.	"This makes no sense. Please rewrite this so that your teacher knows what you're describing."	"Your first sentence is a good overview, but you may want to add transition sentences between paragraphs."

 ## Tip 3: Call The "COPS"

Although modifying her words and tone was helpful, Malia still wanted a step-by-step approach for helping her daughter check her writing independently. She had fallen into the bad habit of correcting Natasha's work for her instead of letting her do it on her own. Unfortunately, this approach didn't foster responsibility and ownership.

In my tutoring practice, with essays and other writing assignments, we teach elementary and middle school kids to use the "COPS" Method. When we say, "Call the COPS!" we're referring to Capitalization, Overall Appearance, Punctuation, and Spelling. Students review one line at a time, looking for all the Cs, then all the Os, and so forth.

C =	CAPITALIZATION	What to capitalize?
Titles, Sentences, Quotes, Proper Nouns - the specific name of a person, place, thing, or special group		
O =	OVERALL APPEARANCE	What to look for?
Overall neatness including spacing, margins, indentation of paragraph, and a title		
P =	PUNCTUATION	What to punctuate, and how?
End of sentence punctuation, commas, quotations		
S =	SPELLING	What's the easiest way to check spelling?
If using the computer, use spell check. When the work is hand-written, use a handheld spell checker, such as the Franklin Speller.		

Once your child has completed the edits, take a look. Note any mistakes using "COPS" acronyms in the margins, like this:

Notes	Natasha's Writing Sample
1C 1S	should soda masheens be
1P	allowed in school. In my
1S	opinyun, they definitely should!
1C	schools can make a lot of
	money by selling soda to
	students and teachers during
1P 1C	the school day our school needs
	the money, so I say - YES!

Your notations in the margins identify mistakes but still allow the student to make corrections independently. For example, in the first line, Natasha had one capitalization mistake and one spelling mistake. Therefore, Maila jotted "1C" and "1S" in the margin so that her daughter would know which mistakes to target. Remember, during the editing process, your child should hold the pencil about 95 percent of the time.

📌 Tip 4: Edit AFTER A Break

Another idea that worked well for Natasha was to begin the editing process after she took a break from her writing assignment. Have you ever noticed that after you've repeatedly read a document mistakes aren't obvious anymore? The same phenomenon applies to kids. Research demonstrates that children are more likely to identify errors after taking a break from writing. Encourage one round of independent editing and then have your child shift to another assignment or take a break. Natasha found that reviewing her writing with fresh eyes made a big difference.

Tip 5: Offer A Reward

As parents, we want to give our kids effective strategies to slow down, focus a bit more on details, and take time to circle back and check their work. The ultimate goal, however, is to get them to do these things independently. How is this done? By noticing when good things are happening! Malia had been in the habit of taking privileges away when Natasha rushed through her work, but she soon found that offering a reward was more effective and resulted in the desired change.

To help your child slow down and focus, present the strategies you would like to reinforce, such as self-correcting, editing, reading high-lighted directions, etc., and then decide on rewards or small additional privileges that will be available if she uses these strategies. A reward might be baking cookies after dinner, a later bedtime, or another small token to recognize her performance. Remember, be consistent and don't just reward her behavior once or twice; keep going. She'll need weeks of using these strategies before they become a new habit.

The Problem

Sean – A 10th Grader
With Different Priorities

Sean was very bright and had been in gifted classes since the third grade. Still, he rushed through his homework so that he could pursue his main passion—video games. His most recent report card reflected mostly Cs, although he was certainly capable of much better grades. He lacked the motivation to do well, and he felt no need to work to his potential. Sean's saving grace was that he did turn in most of his homework; however, it was often hastily scribbled and a bare bones reflection of his true ability. In the 10th grade, his parents were worried because college was on the horizon.

After meeting with Sean alone, I found him to be an engaging young man, but also a kid with mixed-up priorities. Gaming was so much of a passion that he played video games immediately after arriving home from school until late in the evening. Sean was not mature enough to understand the consequences his current actions would have on his future. He didn't make the connection that his current grades were not going to get him into the college of his choice, Virginia Tech.

Sean's situation was actually quite involved. His family had a number of issues at hand. The first, and most obvious obstacle was that school was taking a back seat to gaming. The not so obvious issue was that Sean was having trouble making and keeping friends. Video games gave him instant companions, those with whom he played on-line, but in reality, he was becoming even more socially isolated. I recommended counseling for Sean and his parents, but he still needed support with his schoolwork. His parents and I worked out a plan.

The Solution

 ### Tip 1: Limit Temptations That Lead To Rushing

Sean had easy access to video games, and that had to change. His parents decided to do two things:

- First, they established Dedicated Homework Time. At most, Sean typically did 30 minutes of homework. His parents agreed to set his DHT for 60 minutes. Although it's likely he had more homework than that, Sean may have resisted any additional time.

- Second, they allowed Sean to choose when he would start DHT, but it had to start in time for him to complete his work by 7 pm. At 7 pm, he was allowed access to video games for two hours.

You may be wondering why Sean's parents didn't take away his gaming unit altogether. This was actually their first inclination. It was finally decided that Sean would probably rebel so strenuously that withholding this privilege would be counterproductive. As is so often the case, too much punishment results in even greater resistance.

 ## Tip 2: Hire Outside Help

All kids yearn for independence, especially adolescents, and as children age, they're less willing to accept parental assistance. In Sean's case, his parents had to intervene. They did an excellent job of setting a daily routine and limiting gaming; however, they quickly found that their offers to help Sean with homework were met with immediate rejection.

I suggested that they keep the role of parent but hire a third party to take the role of teacher. I connected them with a wonderful educator who was able to develop a natural rapport with their son. Sean worked hard for this tutor even though he put a wall up for his parents. Why? Because the tutor wasn't Mom or Dad. It was really that simple: Sean took direction from an objective person because it didn't involve any complicated emotional history.

Chapter 5
Homework Made Simple
Checklist

The Rusher's habits can be changed with simple, proactive strategies. Have you:

- ✓ Established Dedicated Homework Time?
- ✓ Created a DHT menu?
- ✓ Jotted down your expectations before homework starts?
- ✓ Used a timer for brief periods of time?
- ✓ Encouraged the use of color?
- ✓ Praised your child for attention to detail?

Chapter 6

What To Do About The Procrastinator

Goals

In this chapter you will learn to help your Procrastinator by:

- Using a timer or other gadget to help get homework started.

- Developing a homework contract to establish expectations.

- Setting realistic estimates for time necessary to complete tasks.

- Breaking down long-term projects into manageable tasks.

- Utilizing privileges to reward desired behavior.

- Creating written reminders to replace verbal requests and nagging.

Most parents subscribe to the idea, "Never put off till tomorrow what you can do today," but their kids prefer the saying, "Never do today what you can put off until tomorrow." As adults, we see the downside of procrastination – stress (on them and us!), anxiety, nagging, late nights, and family conflict. So many children struggle with the temptation to delay the inevitable – especially when a friend is knocking at the door or their favorite TV show is flickering in the background. Parents just want the homework to get done and, interestingly, many children do as well. Procrastinators often vow that next time they will do better, but these students just don't know how to make changes that last.

Does This Sound Familiar?

Test it Out!	A Usually	B Sometimes	C Rarely
My child waits until after dinner or late in the evening to start homework.			
Homework goes unfinished because he runs out of time.			
He underestimates the time it will take to complete homework assignments.			
My child gets up early to complete homework assignments before school.			
My child works only on assignments that are due the next day.			
My child says he works better under pressure.			
Homework is not started unless I ask him to get to it.			
My child makes excuses for not starting, doing, or completing homework.			
My child earns sub-par grades on work that was hastily completed at the last minute.			
I have to badger my child to get homework done.			

Total number of checks in each column	A	B	C

If you answered "usually" or "sometimes" to most of these questions, this chapter is for you.

Why Students Procrastinate

There are many students—and adults—who put off work until the last minute. Although the reasons behind their tendencies are very different, one thing is for sure – Procrastinators underestimate the time it will take to complete their work and overestimate how long they have to do it. When procrastination impacts academics, students need parental intervention in order to change the behaviors that are limiting their success.

Optimism Prevails

Procrastinators are an incredibly optimistic bunch! I tutored one high school student, who was convinced that he could complete a six-page term paper in just two hours. He had the utmost confidence in his claim, reasoning that he could easily research and write one page every 20 minutes. Although this student's concept of time seems implausible, he is not alone in his theory. Procrastinators almost always think they can work faster than they actually do. They rarely account for unexpected—or even expected—interruptions. Even though most Procrastinators swear by their optimistic schedule, they rarely adhere to it and certainly don't escape feeling anxious as the culminating due date approaches.

Bad Habits Linger

Unfortunately, every time a student puts things off, he reinforces a bad habit and falls deeper into his hole. Procrastinators become skilled in avoidance rather than time management. Some students have been caught up in the cycle of daily procrastination for so long that they know no other way to approach assignments. They miss out on learning how to plan, organize, or break down work into more manageable parts. They also miss out on the satisfaction of crossing a completed task off a carefully crafted "to do" list.

In a 1994 study by Roger Buehler, college students were asked to predict how long it would take them to complete their senior thesis. The average estimate was 34 days, though only 30 percent of the students had actually finished their work by the end of this period. Most students ended up requiring almost an additional month to complete their thesis, for an average of 56 total days. Considering the students in this study were of college age, it's easy to understand why elementary, middle, and high school students have trouble estimating the time homework will take.

Roots Of Procrastination

To Procrastinators, anything is better than initiating or completing homework. Besides the universal sentiment that they'd rather do anything else than homework, I've observed two other main reasons why kids procrastinate. They are either overwhelmed because they're unprepared and lack confidence in their abilities or they believe that they work better under the pressure of an impending deadline.

Overwhelmed And Underprepared

The student who feels overwhelmed and underprepared often feels ill-equipped to tackle his homework. He is unclear about the directions for the assignment or feels like the task is so insurmountable that he'll never get it done. His lack of confidence fuels his apprehension and anxiety. Since it's no fun to feel this way, he tries to put off this unpleasant feeling as long as possible. Procrastination seems like the perfect solution, however, it actually worsens the situation.

Loves The Pressure

Those students who say they work better under pressure may actually be feeling a natural high caused by an adrenaline rush as their deadlines approach. Without a deadline, many feel they cannot muster enough energy to get started. When they are up against a deadline and have no choice other than to "just do it," they complete the task. Did you know anyone guilty of "pulling an all-nighter" in college? How was it that they stayed awake into the wee hours of the morning? You guessed it – adrenaline. It's a common phenomenon and one that many students buy into, but the old adage "better under pressure" simply is not true. Studies demonstrate that students who work under these circumstances typically produce inferior, less accurate work, and ultimately receive lower grades.

Short-term Benefit, Long-term Cost

The positive and negative feelings Procrastinators get from putting off work are almost universal. The majority feel better at first because they dodged an uncomfortable task, but soon they're under added pressure and stress.

Even if the task got done this time, procrastinating has an effect on academic performance down the road. Putting off homework, particularly long-term projects such as term papers or studying for a test, is bound to undermine a student's ability to work to his or her full potential.

Most of us know that badgering kids to do homework ultimately backfires. The nagging approach does not allow children to "own" their problem, to create a schedule, and strategize how to tackle the challenge themselves. Not to worry, though. There are sensible solutions to the problem of procrastination.

Help is On the Way!
Tools for the Procrastinator

The Problem

Julie – A Second Grader Who Needs Help Budgeting Time

Julie is a funny, witty, and precocious little girl who wanted to have it her way or no way at all. As a second grader, and the oldest child in her family, she is new to the homework game and so are her parents. They had already begun to argue about how, when, and where Julie should do her schoolwork.

Julie's teacher gives each student a homework packet on Monday which is due on Friday. This approach seems easy enough, but the problem is that Julie either slaves over the entire packet on Monday, insisting that she complete it all at once, or more frequently, waits until Thursday night to begin. When this occurs, Julie has no homework on the other days, so it is hard for her parents to get her into a regular routine.

After meeting with Julie's parents, Mark and Wendy, it was clear that allowing Julie to cram all her work into one day was creating too much tension, as it was very overwhelming for their daughter to complete so much homework in a short amount of time. More importantly, Julie was missing out on a perfect opportunity to learn how to manage her time. And at such a young age, homework shouldn't start out in such a negative way. Mark and Wendy needed some easy-to-use strategies to make after-school life more peaceful.

The Solution

Tip 1: Establish A Launch Day And Time

There is no better time than the primary grades to ingrain the habit of a daily homework start time. In Julie's case, there was no expectation that homework needed to be done at a certain time on a daily basis, so it was often left until Thursday.

- I suggested to Julie's parents that they use Monday as the "launch day" to plan for the remainder of the week. On Monday, when her mother arrived home from work, Wendy and Julie would review her weekly packet. On the upper right hand corner of each page, they would write the day of the week that Julie was to do the page. For example, the first page would be done on Monday, the second and third pages on Tuesday, etc.

- The next step was to figure out a "launch time" – the time at which Julie would start her homework each day. Because the family kept a monthly calendar with the kids' activities, I had them review the week on Monday and then determine when Julie could start her daily homework. Not surprisingly, each day was slightly different due to sports, lessons, and other commitments. Start times were recorded on the calendar. Julie initialed each notation to solidify the agreement.

A Week At A Glance

Mon	Tue	Wed	Thur	Fri
1 3:30 HW JX 4:30 ballet (Julie) 6 pm soccer (Sam)	2 3:30 dentist (Sam/Julie) 4:30 JX homework	3 4 pm JX homework 6 pm ballet	4 3 pm Spanish (Julie) 4:30 JX homework	5 4 pm playdate at the Smith's house

- Julie was encouraged to check the calendar when she came home from school so that she was aware of her start time that day. By having Julie review the calendar, she became responsible for herself. This approach turned the tables. Mark and Wendy were no longer hounding her at random times. The calendar clearly stated when she was to do her work so there was nothing to argue about.

By spreading her homework out and creating a calendar, Wendy and Mark were teaching their daughter to plan ahead and break down large tasks into smaller chunks. These two simple ideas were highly effective in reducing Julie's tendency to procrastinate.

The tips in Julie's vignette apply to children receiving daily homework, not merely a packet at the beginning of the week. Even though primary grade students do not receive a large volume of work, it's imperative for them to become accustomed to adhering to a general schedule early on. When kids get used to a basic routine, research shows that they are more likely to experience homework success when they're older. The three basic principles are:

Principle # 1 - A short break upon returning home from school or extracurricular activities.

Principle # 2 - An agreed upon start time that will vary depending on the day's schedule.

Principle # 3 - Following up with privileges.

Tip 2: Play Beat The Clock

Beat the Clock is a simple game that has been around for a long time; it works especially well for Procrastinators. I encouraged Julie's parents to introduce the game by saying, "This game is a fun way to get homework done so that you have more time to play." Julie's parents first determined how long it would take her to complete an assignment and then set the timer. They said, "If you can get this worksheet finished before the timer goes off, you earn a sticker. If you collect four stickers this week (Mon-Thurs) then you can pick a fun family activity this weekend." Julie thought Beat the Clock was a great idea. It motivated her to start her homework on time without argument.

Of course, each child's reward will be different. You may find that stickers and a larger reward at the end of the week do not motivate your child. Ask her what she wants to earn, and then negotiate a compromise if her ideas are too lofty.

Beat the Clock is initially used to get kids started and finished, but eventually you'll want to encourage accuracy as well. After awhile, phase out this game so that your child becomes more responsible for completion of homework without your help. Play Beat the Clock most days of the week, not each day, if you feel your child can get started without the use of the timer. If she can, give her a sticker for the day she worked without the game.

The Problem

Alexis – A 7th Grade Perfectionist

Alexis, was a bright, conscientious 7th grader, who had a habit of putting off work that was challenging for her. She took a long time to get settled, particularly if the homework involved writing. If her assignment was to compose a story, she'd sit and think about the details for half an hour

Problem cont.

before she even picked up her pencil. Unless the end result met Alexis' high standards, she couldn't move on. When homework became more difficult, her procrastination worsened. Interestingly, Alexis would gladly start her math homework, as it was easy for her; however, she routinely saved her toughest assignment for last. This become a real source of tension between her and her parents.

The Solution

Tip 1: Make A Workable To Do List

Alexis had fallen into the pattern of completing her easy assignments first but putting off any assignment that created stress until later in the evening.

For Procrastinators like Alexis, who is a perfectionist, and for others whose habit for leaving work until the last minute may be rooted in something other than perfectionism, a different approach to prioritizing daily assignments may be necessary. The Premack Principle, based on psychologist David Premack's research, states that pleasant tasks can be used as a reward for doing unpleasant tasks. This applies to homework in the following ways:

- If your child has only one or two simple assignments, agree on a start time and insist that the work be done before anything else. Homework, typically an unpleasant task, is rewarded with free time, the pleasant task.

- If your student has multiple assignments, coach him to start with a tough task followed by an easy one, and to repeat this sequence (hard, easy, hard, easy). Prompt him to label the order in which he will do the homework (1st, 2nd, 3rd, etc.) next to the assignment in the planner. Often, adults and kids alike will put off the work they don't like to do. By the end of the day, the satisfying tasks are done, but the others are not.

- Following something particularly challenging, encourage your child to take a short break by grabbing a snack, playing with the cat, or shooting some hoops. Avoid screen time because it tends to pull kids into another world and all of the homework momentum will be lost.

- There may be some days when your child is on a roll once she starts to work. It's best to continue this momentum straight through instead of taking a break.

No one task on the list should be more than 30 minutes long. When an undertaking feels overwhelming, individuals are far more likely to procrastinate. Instead, break an extensive assignment into two smaller chunks.

Alexis wasn't too keen on changing her ways, but I got her to agree to change the order in which she completed her work for just two weeks. When the two weeks were up, we met again. Alexis opened her planner and told me how she was organizing her time after school. Instead of starting her writing late at night, she did it before dinner. It was usually the second assignment on her "to do" homework list. The third assignment was typically math. This was her favorite subject; so in essence, it was a reward for completing her writing assignment.

Tip 2: Tackle The Tolerable 10

Timers are great tools for all kinds of homework issues, but for the Procrastinator, they're priceless. If your child has trouble sitting down and focusing, set the timer for just 10 minutes. Knowing that she only has 10 minutes to go can help her overcome the Procrastinator's hesitation to get started. She'll often realize that the task isn't so overwhelming after all, and soon she will be able to work longer.

The Tolerable 10 was Alexis' favorite strategy when it came to any work involving writing. She found that when she simply started the work she was able to keep going.

There are many timers available on the market, but my favorite is the Time Timer (www.timetimer.com) shown here. It helps kids understand the concept of elapsed time by providing a visual depiction. Another kid-friendly option is the Time Tracker (www.learningresources.com). This device shows elapsed time digitally and also has colored lights and sound effects. Less expensive kitchen timers are also effective, but be sure to purchase one with a clock face. This visual is better for gaining a comprehension of time.

Tip 3: Set A Completion Deadline

Alexis frequently edited, revised, and reviewed her work far more than was necessary. Sometimes, she would stay up until 10 pm – too late for a student her age.

Procrastinators, whether they have perfectionist tendencies or not, should have a daily deadline for homework completion. I recommend that homework be finished at least half an hour before bedtime. In Alexis' case, this deadline limited her propensity to make revisions in search of the perfect paper. Ultimately, she was never totally happy with the end result. The half hour before bedtime rule helps all Procrastinators by:

- Eliminating the problem of late night homework because the student started belatedly in the first place. When kids say, "Mom, I have to stay up later because I need to finish this science lab," most parents are so happy that the child is actually doing the work that they allow this practice on a regular basis. Set this rule and adhere to it by stating, "Lights off at 10 pm, so homework needs to be done by 9:30. Please put everything away then."

- Allowing students to get an adequate amount of sleep. Many teens get a second wind late at night and work into the wee hours. Although this change in sleeping pattern is part of normal development during adolescence, many kids push late nights to the limit. Children between the ages of seven and twelve need at least 10 hours of sleep, and teens require approximately 8-1/2 hours of sleep per night. By setting a completion deadline, you may find your child falling asleep earlier.

The Problem

Ian – A 9th Grade Dawdler

Ian was a high school student who typically spent his study hall doodling and looking through automobile magazines. As a car enthusiast and wannabe mechanic, Ian justified his actions by telling himself that this research was essential to his career development plan. His father, Jim, reported that Ian's chronic dawdling was driving him crazy. Because Jim worked out of his house, he was able to directly observe Ian's method of operation, which included watching TV after school, the auto channel of course, and then tinkering outside in the tool shed until dinner. Even after dinner, Ian was slow to start.

When Jim asked his son, "Do you have homework?" Ian typically replied, "Yeah, I'll do it later." Some nights, he wouldn't even begin until 10 pm. It often took the threat of restriction before he would finally sit down. Both Jim and his wife were frustrated with their son, and Ian was tired of his parents' badgering and threats as well.

Jim complained that his son was never on top of his homework and had countless excuses not to do the work right away. It's always, "after this show is over," or " after I get to the next level of this video game."

In elementary school, Ian's homework wasn't a problem because the assignments were basic and brief. When he got to middle school, and the assignments became more complex, his grades began to fall. Now, in high school, he managed to be a solid C student, but his parents were convinced he could do better if they could help to curb his procrastination.

The Solution

 Tip 1: Ask The Right Questions

After a few visits with Ian and his parents, I noticed that Jim was particularly upset by Ian's response when asked if he had homework. I suggested that he eliminate the question, "Do you have homework?" and replace it with "What do you have to do tonight?" and "When will you do it?" It's been my experience that when kids can answer both of these questions, much of our work is done.

"What do you have to do tonight?" – When Ian arrived home from school, Jim would ask the question. He requested to see Ian's planner so that they could have a quick two-minute conversation regarding the day's assignments. Jim realized that when he talked too much, Ian would tune out.

The next question - **"When will you do it?"** – helped Ian start thinking about when he would start his work. Even though Ian didn't have a packed schedule, he did play in the school band, which required after-school practices twice each week. The time at which he started his homework varied, so his father decided to use the Time Management Chart (TMC) I suggested.

On the Monday they began this new approach, Jim sat down with Ian and explained that having a schedule in writing will help them both remember when homework would be done. Ian first recorded his extracurricular activities. Then he chose homework blocks in 30 minute increments that worked for him. The only rule that Jim had was that homework had to be started before dinner and completed a half hour prior to bedtime. The same held true for weekends, except that Ian could choose the day (Friday, Saturday, or Sunday) on which he'd do the work. After the TMC was finished, Ian posted it in his dad's home office, which was where they touched base after school. Each Monday Ian and his dad would create a new TMC because his schedule often varied from week to week. Although there were certainly changes that weren't anticipated (doctor's appointments, an extra band practice, etc.), the TMC provided a general weekly outline and greatly reduced Ian's temptation to put off homework.

Weekly Schedule — For the week of 10-5

Time	Mon	Tue	Wed	Thur	Fri/Sat/Sun (choose one)
3:30-4:00	break	band practice	break	band practice	
4:00-4:30	↓				
4:30-5:00	↓				
5:00-5:30	Art class	↓	↓	↓	
5:30-6:00	↓	break	HW	break	HW
6:00-6:30	HW	HW	HW	HW	HW
6:30-7:00	dinner	dinner	dinner	dinner	dinner
7:00-7:30	chores	chores	chores	chores	Chores
7:30-8:00	HW	HW	HW	HW	free time
8:00-8:30	HW	HW	free time	HW	
8:30-9:00	free time	free time	↓	free time	
9:00-9:30	↓	↓	↓	↓	↓

Tip 2: Record Homework Start Time In The Planner

After a month, Ian fell into a more predictable routine. The TMC wasn't needed as much. Jim's inclination was to let Ian function completely on his own at this point, but I felt it was too early. I advised him to continue to ask the same questions, "What do you have to do tonight?" and "When will you do it?" But instead of a formal TMC, Jim asked Ian to simply write the time at which he was going to start homework in his planner. When they met after school, he and Ian briefly discussed the day's agenda, and Ian recorded his start time next to the assignment he was going to begin first. By doing so, Ian was better able to manage his time and work more efficiently.

Eventually these written schedules may not be necessary, but it's important in the beginning to establish good habits. Ian's parents saw a big difference in his "I'll do it later" attitude when they insisted on a regular start time and didn't allow tinkering in the tool shed until his work was completed. Although they were inclined to take away his car magazines and tools completely, they knew that without them, they'd have no leverage. This minor change produced significant returns.

Tip 3: Reward An On-time Start

Once Ian got started on his homework, he was able to finish it independently, but sometimes, he lacked the initiative to begin. In the past, Jim yelled at his son when he found him dawdling. But this time around, Jim took the opposite route – he rewarded Ian for an on-time start. When Ian began at the time that was recorded on the TMC or his planner, Jim put a dollar in a jar. Ian was allowed to use the money to buy mechanic's tools, but the money could only be used for this purpose.

Rewarding your child for starting on time is far better than punishing him for not. If procrastination has been chronic and seemingly insurmountable, give a reward for simply beginning the work on time. The reward doesn't have to be money; it can be a later bedtime, extended curfew, or additional screen time. Ask your child what he's willing to work for, within reason, of course – he'll let you know! Another option is the simple acknowledgement of starting on time. Genuine praise is a non-tangible reward that goes a long way.

Tip 4: Fade The Daily Meetings And Rewards

When you find that your child is able to start on time without much prompting from you, it's time to step back. Do this gradually. In Ian's case, his father continued to ask the same two questions daily, but he only asked to see his planner two days per week. After another month, Jim did not review it with Ian at all unless he had an inclination that Ian wasn't being forthcoming about his workload.

As time went on, Jim cut down on the monetary rewards. They developed an agreement that if Ian only had to be reminded once during the week to start his homework, Jim would give him $5 for the week. Eventually, Ian decided that "the money wasn't really important" and that he'd rather work on his own than have his dad checking on him.

The Problem

Marcus – A 5th Grader Who Had Trouble Planning Ahead

On a cold January morning, I received an email from a former client of mine, Dawn. She said in no uncertain terms that she had had it with her son's habit of waiting until the last minute to work on projects. I hadn't spoken to Dawn in a couple of years. She and I worked together to tackle some other homework issues when her son was in third grade. At that time, Marcus was procrastinating mainly because he didn't know where to start. He felt overwhelmed by homework even at an early age. I taught him how to prioritize his assignments in his planner each day, and Dawn implemented "Beat the Clock" and a few other strategies that I suggested.

This time around, Marcus' problem wasn't daily homework. He was actually doing quite well and had become a fairly independent learner. The problem was the assignments that were not due the next day – book reports, science projects, and even tests. At 9 pm the night before (Tuesday), Marcus informed Dawn that he had a book report due on Friday and had not even chosen a book. This wasn't the first time Marcus pulled such a stunt; in fact, it was the second time that month. Marcus had no idea how to plan ahead, and his mother didn't know how to teach him.

Marcus and Dawn came to see me later that week. For an hour, we worked together. We started by sifting through his binder to figure out which long-term assignments were on the horizon. He had two projects (his teacher loved projects) due later that month. I asked him why he didn't write the information down in his planner. He replied, "I can't. These aren't due tomorrow. My planner is only for stuff like homework." As with many kids, Marcus didn't see long-term assignments as homework, and that was the root of his problem.

The Solution

 ### Tip 1: Create A False Sense Of Urgency

Procrastination is a coping mechanism that actually works for homework that is due the next day. When a student knows a task absolutely has to get done, his sense of urgency is heightened. He gets into gear and completes the work. But this approach is rarely successful for assignments that require multiple steps. When layers of work are involved, putting off one part has a ripple effect which throws the entire project out of kilter.

- The first step for tackling long-term assignments is to break the big assignment into small tasks. Depending on complexity, your child may want to aim for four to seven small chunks that lead up to the final product.

- Next, assist him with creating a false sense of urgency using interim deadlines for each task. These incremental task deadlines give some kids a mechanism for arousal they may not naturally possess.

- Lastly, be sure the tasks associated with the deadlines are specific. If they are vague, students are less likely to tackle the work. Specific tasks equal action, not procrastination.

Specific Terms = Action	Vague Words = Procrastination
Write thesis statement and two paragraphs	Write rough draft

Specific Terms = Action	Vague Words = Procrastination
Make 15 Smart Cards	Learn vocab words
Review and recite study guide answers	Study for test

Because Marcus wasn't utilizing his planner at all for long-term work, he was easy to help. There weren't any bad habits to correct. I showed him how to take an upcoming geography project, break it into small steps and determine when he'd have to do each step to finish the project on time. He recorded these steps in his planner - an important part of this strategy.

As we worked through the process, Marcus' first inclination was to jot down completion tasks using vague words. For example, one of the steps needed to complete the geography project was to trace a map from a page in his text book. He merely wrote "draw map." This wasn't nearly descriptive enough. It's likely that Marcus would have either forgotten what to do or been overwhelmed by the seemingly large task at hand. We reworded his notation to read, "trace map on pg. 157."

 ## Tip 2: Make Long-term Tasks Part Of Daily Homework

The payoff to recording long-term tasks in the planner is that they become part of the daily homework list. Check out Marcus' new and improved planner. Notice the way he precisely recorded how he would study for his science test scheduled for Friday. He was very specific about the steps needed to prepare for the exam. Now these smaller assignments are prioritized along with the regular daily homework.

The final step for Marcus is to prioritize all the tasks in the order in which he'll do them. It's as simple as numbering each one – 1, 2, 3, etc. Now, there is no longer stress over an impending project or test. Marcus got the hang of this concept quickly and admitted that he "liked writing it down better than having to remember all the stuff."

Marcus' Planner

	Wed	Thurs	Fri
MATH	Finish review package ③	Study-do ① practice probs. on pg. 64	MATH QUIZ
SOCIAL STUDIES	Paste ② diagrams and label	Color and proofread writing on poster ②	POSTER PROJECT DUE
SCIENCE	Make 20 vocab ① flashcards	Review study guide w/mom ④ & dad	TEST
LANGUAGE ARTS	④ Read Chapter 8	③ Read chapter 9 and questions	NONE

In the beginning, your child will need your help to plan ahead. If you find that he is able to do this independently, update information with him regularly - try for once a week during Clean Sweep maintenance described on page 79.

Tip 3: Incorporate Fun Into Project Planning

Dawn and Marcus found great success with Tip 2. Marcus' planning skills were much improved. However, some of his projects were very time-consuming and required up-front work such as purchasing or gathering the correct supplies. These steps weren't necessarily assignments that could be recorded in the planner, but they were certainly part of the preparation process. I suggested another twist that they could incorporate when needed – the Tootsie Roll® Planning Guide, especially since Marcus responded well to rewards.

- Using a giant Tootsie Roll® (the kind you can buy at the movie theatre) and the following guide, determine the six steps necessary to complete the project and their corresponding due dates.

- Cut the Tootsie Roll® into six pieces. Each time your child completes a step, reward him with a piece of the candy.

Tootsie Roll® Project Planning Guide

Title of Project: Helen of Troy   *Due Date:* October 1

Supplies and Materials:

- White poster board
- Glue
- Magic markers
- Scissors
- Helen of Troy book

Brain storm 5 key facts	Find pictures and copy	Layout and glue materials	Glue pics	Decorate poster board	Hand in at school
Do it on 9/21	Do it on 9/23	Do it on 9/25	Do it on 9/28	Do it on 9/29	Do it on 10/1

I will follow this plan in order to complete to my project on time. When I'm done with each step, I will show my parents and cut off a section of the Tootsie Roll® to eat.

George Schwartz
Student Signature

I will check in with my child on the above dates. Other than that, I will not provide assistance unless asked.

Mary Ann Schwartz
Parent Signature

Project Planning Guide

Title of Project: Science Fair Project **Date:** Nov. 17

Supplies Needed:

Poster display board	Newspaper
Stencils	Flour
Marker	Water
Glue Stick	Paint

"To Do" Steps	Complete On
Decide on topic	Oct. 12
Do background research	Oct. 19
Purchase materials	Oct. 20
Set up project	Oct. 27
Collect data	Nov. 1
Prepare project display	Nov. 9
Write oral presentation	Nov. 12
Practice oral presentation	Nov. 15

I will follow this plan in order to complete my project on time and will show work to my parents each Friday. I will ask for help when needed.

X _____ Cathy O'Brian _____

Student Signature

I will only offer advice when asked. If work is completed each Friday, then I agree to a later curfew on Saturday night.

X _____ Majorie O'Brian _____

Parents Signature

The Problem

Colin and Caitlin - Siblings Who Had Trouble With Time

Colin and Caitlin Simpson were fourth and sixth graders who had one thing in common – the concept of time was completely alien to them, especially when it came to homework. Both children constantly started homework too late in the day to be ready for their evening activities.

The day usually went like this – both children would arrive home to their babysitter, Susanna. They'd get a snack and jump right on the computer or grab an iPod. When Susanna reminded them that they needed to start their homework, she heard, "I hardly have any. It will only take me 20 minutes!" or "I'll have plenty of time to do it later." The reminders turned into begging. Finally, just before dinner, the kids began to work. After about 15 minutes, they typically realized that they had far more work than anticipated, but it was too late. At 5:30 they had to leave the house – Colin had basketball practice and Caitlin was dropped off at gymnastics. When they arrived back home, it was 7 pm, about the same time their parents were returning from work. Mr. and Mrs. Simpson were increasingly frustrated and disappointed to learn that their children still had plenty of homework left to do.

In working with this family, it was quickly apparent that there were two main issues in play. The first was that the children were unable to predict the amount of time their homework would take. The second was that Susanna had little control over getting the children to initiate homework. I initially helped them to deal with the situation by establishing Designated Homework Time. This was implemented to be sure the majority of work was completed before they had to leave for their extracurricular activities. The next steps were to teach the children better time estimation skills and to draft contracts to set boundaries and limits.

The Solution

Tip 1: Become An Expert Time Estimator

Just like Colin and Caitlin, Procrastinators overestimate the time they have to complete homework and underestimate how long it will take. For one reason or another, their sense of time is off. You can use any of these three methods to help your child become a better estimator of time.

For younger students:

Method #1

- Ask your child how long she thinks it will take her to complete her assignment.

- Jot her reply on the top corner of her paper.

- Set the timer and have her begin.

- Afterward, record the actual time underneath the estimated time.

Discuss any discrepancy with her, explaining that the time needed for an assignment can be hard to predict, so budgeting extra time into her schedule will help her succeed.

Method #2

Use a three-column chart similar to the one on the following page so your child can see her tendency to overestimate or underestimate the time needed.

Task	Estimated Time	Actual Time
10 spelling sentences	10 minutes	23 minutes
Math worksheet	15 minutes	24 minutes

For older students:

Method #3

Older students can get a better grip on time by recording their estimated and actual times independently. As they prioritize their assignments in the planner, they can also write down how long the tasks might take. This worked well with the siblings. When they arrived home from school, Susanna asked them to open their planners. They were expected to number their assignments in the order in which they'd do the work and then, next to each assignment, they recorded how long they felt the work would take. Susanna took a few minutes after they finished their DHT to discuss the accuracy of their estimates. She found that they became increasingly more precise after just a week. The process of prioritizing and estimating accomplished three goals. It helped the students:

- Realize they had been underestimating the time required to complete homework.

- Agree to start homework earlier in the day. This allowed them to spend more quality time with their parents in the evening.

- Develop their time management skills.

Tip 2: Develop A Homework Agreement To Curb Procrastination

A homework agreement is a written contract between adult and student. It spells out exactly what the student and the adult agree to, lists rewards for achieving these goals, and identifies consequences for not living up to the agreement. An agreement clarifies expectations. You'll hear less of "You didn't tell me that!" or "That's not fair!"

The sample agreement that follows was used for Colin and Caitlin. I suggested that the family use this tool because the children needed very specific incentives and consequences. Expectations between the parents and the babysitter were very different. When they began using a written agreement, everyone was on the same page.

The children did not like the idea at first, but the adults stood their ground. After two weeks, they agreed to renegotiate the document with the kids. I felt this was a reasonable time frame to get the children used to having consistent expectations day in and day out. It also gave them something to look forward to. When the two weeks were up, Colin and Caitlin gave their input but did not request drastic changes.

This contract was specific to Colin and Caitlin's issues with estimating time and beginning homework earlier in the day. The agreement you develop can be modified based on your situation. Keep the following ideas in mind when drafting your own agreement.

- Identify the most significant behavior. If it's breaking down long-term tasks, start there.

- List just a few rules, no more than four or five. In order to increase compliance, be sure the rewards outweigh the consequences.

Homework Agreement

This agreement is between Colin, Caitlin, Mom, Dad, and Susanna.

Colin and Caitlin agree to these three tasks:

- Begin homework ½ hour after arriving home from school.
- Jot down an estimate of how long each assignment will take.
- Complete homework or study during 50 minutes of daily Dedicated Homework Time (DHT).

The adults agree to:

- Provide a ½ hour break after school.
- Assist with homework when asked.
- Provide screen time as follows:

    - 20 minutes for beginning homework on time.
    - 20 minutes for recording an estimated time for each assignment.
    - 20 minutes for completing DHT.

- If Colin and Caitlin complete all three tasks three out of four days (Monday thru Thursday), they are allowed to spin the spinner on Friday for a bonus reward.

This contract is to be reviewed in 2 weeks.

Signed __*Colin*__   Signed __*Caitlin*__

Signed __*Ellen*__   Signed __*Peter*__

Signed __*Susanna*__

- Be sure there is a daily reward for your child. You may also wish to include a larger incentive for the end of the week. For example, if he adheres to the agreement four out of five days, he can have a sleepover.

- A creative and motivating way to give this weekly reward is to use a homemade spinner. You can find an easy template on the internet or at www.reallygoodstuff.com. Fill the blanks with rewards that interest your child. In order to keep the suspense, you'll want to vary the incentives monthly.

- Finally, step back. By agreeing to the contract, you have put the ball in your child's court. Praise him when he's doing what he's supposed to do. Resist the inclination to correct him if he's not following through; that is why there are consequences in place.

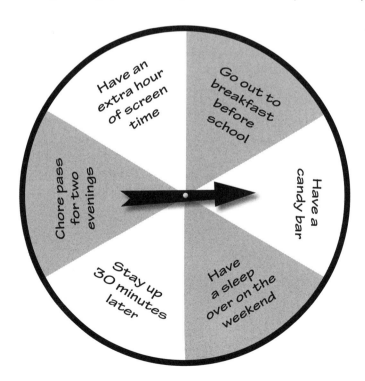

Tip 3: Use A Monthly Calendar

Another common issue that affected the Simpson family was ke
track of long-term assignments. It's tricky enough with one child. W
you have two, three, or more children all receiving projects from n
tiple teachers, finding a way to monitor these tasks is essential. Earl,
in this chapter, I described how Marcus used his planner to plan h
work. Another option is to use a monthly calendar to track long-term
projects. Have your child list the final due date for each assignment
and then record the incremental steps needed to complete it. Consider
color coding the calendar using a single color for each child.

Monthly Calendar

Sun	Mon	Tue	Wed	Thur	Fri	Sat
1	2	3 Start study guide 1-15	4 Study guide 16-30	5 MATH TEST	6	7
8 Put vocab on 3 x 5 card	9 Start reviewing vocab	10 Have mom test study guide	11 HISTORY TEST	12 Start-Pick topic, choose 5 sources	13 Create outline	14
15 Complete rough draft	16 Edit final copy Call COPS	17 ENGLISH ESSAY DUE	18	19 Write hypothesis	20 Create outline	21
22	23 Type findings	24 Put display on board	25 Bring to school	26 SCIENCE PROJECT DUE!	27	28
29	30 Finish draft	1 Final copy	2 PAPER DUE	3	4	5

The key to staying on top of long-term planning is to make it a part of your weekly maintenance meeting. Just as your child will organize his materials, he can also work on organizing his time. Initially, you'll need to help him enter these assignments onto a calendar. Once it becomes part of the weekly routine, he'll be able to take greater ownership.

Chapter 6
Homework Made Simple
Checklist

The Procrastinator's habits can be modified with these simple strategies. Have you:

- ✓ Completed a Time Management Chart with your child?

- ✓ Rewarded him or her for an on-time start?

- ✓ Used a timer for the Tolerable 10 or Beat the Clock?

- ✓ Helped your child become a better estimator of time?

- ✓ Drafted a homework agreement?

- ✓ Encouraged the use of a planner or monthly calendar for long-term work?

Chapter 7

What To Do About The Avoider

Goals

In this chapter you will learn to:

- Stop the persistent cycle of homework avoidance.

- Reduce or eliminate arguments over homework.

- Identify homework trouble spots.

- Develop a written homework agreement.

- Seek help from the right source when all else fails.

Many students procrastinate when it comes to starting homework they find unappealing or difficult to do. Some kids just try to avoid it altogether. Whereas the Procrastinator will eventually do his work, the Avoider refuses to even think about starting the task at hand. These kids stymie their parents and teachers and disappoint themselves. Avoidant behavior is perhaps the most challenging homework issue discussed in this book.

Avoiders Often:

- Claim they have no homework or insist it was done in school.

- Lie about assignments and the poor grades they have received.

- Seem unaware of assignments even when they're posted on the school's website.

- "Forget" to bring home the necessary materials to complete work.

Does This Sound Familiar?

Test it out!	A Usually	B Sometimes	C Rarely
My child claims to have little to no homework day in and day out.			
She has many reasons and excuses about why there is no homework.			
My child says homework is completed, but it really is not.			
I battle with my child over starting and completing homework.			
Teachers have told me that report card grades would be better if homework was consistently completed and turned in.			
My child is more likely to complete basic assignments rather than the ones that require planning and diligence.			
She doesn't write down the homework the teacher assigns.			
My child forgets to bring her assignment notebook and other materials home from school.			
My interventions have not helped to improve the behavior.			

Total number of checks in each column	A	B	C

If you answered "usually" or "sometimes" to the majority of these questions, this chapter is for you.

The Common Thread

Many students who fit the Avoider profile are considered "unmotivated" by their parents and teachers. The façade they present is strikingly similar. These students seem as if they do not care about school, but deep down, they have the desire to do better. Some Avoiders feel that there is no need to exert effort because they are never going to do well. Once children become accustomed to this pattern of behavior, it takes serious work to help them overcome their feelings of helplessness.

With Avoiders, parents and teachers face two serious obstacles: deep-seated self-doubt and poor work habits. Over the years, I've taught many students who had no idea how to set up an organized binder, prioritize their assignments, and plan ahead. "Studying" for a test consisted of merely glancing over the chapter. When the time came, they were sadly unprepared for advanced classes and college.

A Hole Dug Too Deep

Students avoid homework for many reasons. One of the most common reasons is a feeling of helplessness which worsens over time. In the early grades, these children may struggle academically and see no pay-off regardless of their effort. They feel that no matter how hard they try, they cannot meet the expectations of their teachers, parents, and even themselves. When they do earn a good grade, they don't make the connection between the work put into achieving it and the end result. When Avoiders do take the time to study, they often attribute their good grade to luck, not from the effort they put into it. As a result, an "A" or "B" here or there doesn't change their outlook. Instead, they need a steady diet of success.

Keeping up with their peers academically requires a tremendous amount of effort. Many of these kids have an undiagnosed learning disability or attention disorder, but parents and teachers may not realize this. They feel that the students' poor work quality is a result of not trying hard enough or a lack of motivation. As these children age, they develop a serious aversion to homework due to years of academic struggle. What starts out as procrastination and whining, evolves into lying about work that's due and sometimes defiant refusal to do any work at all.

Locked In A Battle Of Wills

In addition to the Avoiders discussed above, there is another small group, usually adolescents, who gain satisfaction from pushing their parents' buttons. In attempts to help their child succeed, parents can unknowingly exert too much control. This can lead to power struggles between the child and parents, and sometimes with teachers or other adults. When power struggles are constant, children may disengage and refuse to abide by certain rules or expectations. After all, the areas of life that they directly control are homework, grades, and behavior.

I'm At The End Of My Rope!

Whatever the reason for avoidance – a learning or attention difficulty, a power struggle, or simply a lack of appreciation for the value of a good education – it must be dealt with immediately. Waiting for a turnaround can lead to the avoidant behaviors becoming worse over time. Continuing power struggles can be a destructive force in family dynamics, potentially leading to generalized anxiety and/or other mental health issues. Some experts say that these mental health disorders are often the primary cause of homework avoidance in the first place. In any case, without prompt parental and professional involvement, improvement may never occur.

Some of the most difficult students I have worked with were those whose problems had festered for years without significant intervention. Their academic "hole" was so deep, and their negative attitudes were so ingrained, that it took much more time for change to take place. That's why it's imperative to tackle this issue head-on as early as possible. Positive parental involvement is a must. These children can be tough to love at times, but stay the course. As one of my favorite authors, Rick Lavoie, says, "Kids need love most when they deserve it least."

HELP IS ON THE WAY!
TOOLS FOR THE AVOIDER

The Problem

David – A Fifth Grade Boy With Frustrated Parents

David Karnes' parents and teachers labeled him as "unmotivated," but David was certainly eager – just not when it came to homework. A fifth grader with an analytical mind of someone twice his age, David skirted assignments that were, in his words, "boring." Instead of cracking open his books after school, David just wanted to surf the internet and listen to music in his room. Although he avoided homework in all subjects but his favorite, math, David earned passing grades. He was incredibly bright, so he managed to earn Bs and Cs on quizzes and tests, but received lower report card grades due to missing homework.

David's parents, Carrie and John, wished they had a dime for every teacher who said, "David is a smart boy, if only he'd apply himself." Their constant nagging did little to help. John said, "When we're unrelenting, asking about homework and checking in, he seems to do better. But the minute we back off, he's back to the same old habits."

John and Carrie wanted desperately for their son to take a greater interest in school. They made the mistake of thinking that the more they stayed on his case, the better he'd do. This was true for the short-term, but didn't work long-term. The other mistake they made was taking away the things that David enjoyed at the first hint of a bad grade. When I first met the Karnes' family, David had been restricted from his iPod, TV, computer, and even playing outside with his friends. He had become even more rebellious.

The Solution

 ## Tip 1: Give SOME Control Back

Serious Avoiders often feel like they are driving down a road without their hands on the steering wheel. They don't perceive that they have control over their own life, so they rebel by controlling anything that's within their grasp - most often schoolwork. As a classroom teacher and tutor, I experienced the most success with my students when I allowed them to take the reins from time to time. I tried to treat them like the young adults they were and not like little children. The majority of students appreciate being asked, not always told. I encouraged David's parents to ask for their son's input regarding schoolwork.

Allowing kids to have a say in their after-school schedule is important. Just like the Procrastinator, the Avoider needs an after-school schedule. But with the Avoider, it works best if it's on his terms.

David's mother decided to use the Time Management Chart on page 121 so that David could have some control over his schedule. As he filled in his after-school commitments, Carrie asked questions like, "What's the earliest time you might consider starting?" or "When can you fit in your first block of homework?" Sometimes, she found that the answer wasn't always what she wanted to hear, but nine times out of ten his responses were appropriate. Avoiders are far less likely to risk failure if they are the ones who come up with the solutions.

 ## Tip 2: Break The Cycle Of Negativity

There is always a black cloud called homework hanging over the Avoiders. More than any other group, these kids have associated loathing, despair, and failure with homework. As parents, we have to find a way to break this cycle of negativity. This starts by making homework as pleasurable as possible. I gave Carrie and John the following suggestions:

- First, change YOUR mindset. The moment you return home from work or your child enters the door after school, always greet him with a smile. Keep the mood light; don't pepper him with questions about his school day. Instead, give him some time to relax and then ask about homework.

- Play music in the background. Not only does instrumental music lighten the mood, it also helps kids pay attention.

- Play a game. Think to yourself, "How can I make this more fun?" Is there one assignment on the list that can be transformed from dull to delightful? See pages 178 & 207 for a host of novel ideas.

- Let him be the teacher. Astonishingly, allowing the student to take the role of the teacher helps improve retention of information and focus. If he has an upcoming test, have him teach you the concepts instead of you quizzing him. Ask him to give you some practice problems. See if you can solve them, but more importantly, let him correct you. David's mom found that this technique worked like a charm. Her son, who was generally quiet and reserved, came alive when he finally got to be the teacher!

- Invite a friend over. A study buddy is an excellent way to engage your child in homework. Identify the specific assignment, and have him call a friend to do it with him. Set ground rules first and limit the visit to no more than an hour.

- When previewing assignments with your child, try to determine the teacher's objective. For example, if your child has difficulty with reading and is required to read a section in his science text and answer four related questions, offer to read the text to him or with him so that he can more easily absorb the information. Encourage him complete the written part independently. It is likely that the teacher's goal is for her students to master the science content, not to improve reading fluency skills. This approach eliminates one obstacle that Avoiders often encounter.

 ## Tip 3: Notice Little Improvements

When battles over homework intensified, Carrie and John had the inclination to scold and admonish David. For example, one day he proclaimed that he had no homework – once again. Carrie yelled, "What do you mean you have no homework? No wonder your grades are Cs and Ds! If only you could apply yourself!" Eventually, she and John came to the conclusion that this reaction only exacerbated the problem and pushed David further away.

I advised them to turn the tables and take a totally different approach when talking with their son. David was feeling so poorly about learning, modifying his outlook was first and foremost. He clearly had strengths, but there were very few positives in his school career. After some trial and error, his parents learned to accentuate the positive, even if they were minor accomplishments.

Scenario	Do's	Don'ts
David completed his math homework, but it was barely legible.	Make a big deal over the fact that he finished it. He's done – put it away.	Tell him you're glad he's finished, but it's too messy. He's to rewrite the problems you can't read.
Only half of his science lab was done by 11 pm.	Praise him for finishing half of it (it's half more than he usually does). He can hand it in this way.	Insist that he finish the entire lab.
He recorded most of his homework in his planner, but forgot what was due in English.	Commend the initiative he took. This is a huge step since he refused to write it down in the past. After the other work is started, encourage him to check online for the English assignment.	Focus on the fact that he still does not know what he has for English homework. Badger him until he figures it out.

In praising your child, be genuine, but don't feel the need to lavish praise unnecessarily. Kids can read between the lines and know when insincere words are used as an attempt to change their behavior. Give praise when it's due, especially when related to effort.

 ## Tip 4: Say "Yes" More Often

"Can I text my friends?"

"Can I play video games?"

"Can I go over to Alex's house – just for a half hour?"

David's parents' natural response was, "No, not until you're homework is done!"

Their reasoning was that privileges shouldn't come until homework is finished. Although this concept is generally true, the way it's said makes a big difference in the child's attitude and his willingness to complete the work. Instead of saying "no," respond with "yes." By doing so, you're accentuating the payoff, not the fact that he still has to do homework. This simple approach will improve your child's attitude and decrease power struggles. Shift "no" to "yes" this way:

"Can I text my friends?"
"Yes, you can have your phone just as soon as your math is done."

"Can I play video games?"
"You sure can! Just finish that spelling first."

"Can I go over to Alex's house – just for a half hour?"
"Yes, you may. Complete those science questions and you're free to go."

The Problem

Darius – A Middle Schooler Who Wasn't Always Forthcoming

Darius was a shy kid who did well in class when he connected with the teacher. When he didn't like the teacher – watch out. He put forth very little effort and rarely completed homework, uttering, "I don't have any." From talking with neighborhood friends, Darius' mom knew that the teachers were definitely assigning homework and she was concerned that her son wasn't doing it.

To make matters worse, Darius was experiencing full-blown adolescent rebellion. At 14 years of age, he was walking a fine line between wanting his mother's help and desiring complete independence. When he asked his mother for help with a history assignment, she'd assist him but no matter what she said, it wasn't right. He'd push her away almost immediately. Darius had a tough time accepting help, even when he needed it most.

When I first met Darius Jones, he said all of ten words to me in half an hour. He came across as timid and shy, but I knew from speaking with his parents that he'd come out of his shell. It took a few sessions, but Darius finally opened up to me. I quickly found out that he didn't want to have anything to do with homework and saw no reason for it. He felt that he'd been slighted by some of his teachers who gave far more work than his friends' teachers. "It's not fair!" was the common theme throughout our sessions. "Yes, it's true," I stated, "Life is inherently unfair. That's just how it goes sometimes. Let's talk about ways to make it easier for you."

In Darius' case, there were certain negotiables and non-negotiables. There were some things on which I advised his parents to compromise, and some that required standing firm. One negotiable was accepting help – he could request it when needed and Mom would agree to assist. But Mom agreed not to hover, only to help when asked. The other negotiable was when and where he did homework, as long as he got it done. Although one solution for Darius was setting up a Designated Homework Time, we let him pick the start time and location. The non-negotiables were actually doing the homework and keeping his planner up-to-date with the correct assignments. In order to improve success with the non-negotiables, I suggested that Darius' parents employ the following strategies:

The Solution

Tip 1: Establish Designated Homework Time

Darius was a master of excuses. His parents said, "He has a million and one reasons why he doesn't have any homework." They usually found out this wasn't true. By instituting Designated Homework Time (DHT), Darius and his parents agreed and adhered to a block of 60 minutes for homework, Monday through Thursday. By setting up DHT, they sent the message that he had to set aside a portion of the day for homework, regardless of how little work he said he had. Take a look at page 91 to figure out your child's time allotment based on grade level.

As you can imagine, Darius wasn't keen on this idea. He told his parents he was going to change his ways immediately and really didn't need so much oversight. They were aware that this might happen, but stood their ground, refusing to get into this verbal battle with Darius. They knew that sticking to DHT was key to restoring family harmony and academic success.

Tip 2: Access Online Homework Postings

Once Designated Homework Time took root, study time was much smoother. There was still one unresolved issue; Darius wasn't always forthcoming about his workload. There were a number of assignments that Darius failed to record in his planner which did not get done. His parents weren't aware of the incomplete work until they received his interim report or got a call from his teacher.

Most school districts have invested in technology that enables teachers to post their daily assignments online. These web-based platforms are an excellent way for students and their parents to obtain clarification of homework. Not only do teachers keep lists of what they've assigned that day, but they also post information regarding projects, tests, and other long-term coursework that may be just around the bend. In addition, students can download worksheets and other papers that they may have forgotten at school. This technology is an excellent tool for kids to keep abreast of their assignments and for parents who simply want to know what's going on in the classroom.

If you think the information your child has recorded in his planner is inaccurate or incomplete, have him pull up the course information and print out the daily assignments. This method isn't foolproof, because not all teachers post their homework daily, but it is still a great way to stay in the loop.

It may be tempting to log on to see what your child has for homework that evening, especially if he reports that he has none, but resist the urge. This is your child's responsibility. Have him gather the information and print it out for you. I've worked with many parents who routinely monitor their child's assignments this way. The problem is that the student never learns to record his assignments in class or retrieve them online independently. Feel free to check from time to time, but keep in mind that it is not your job to get this information for your child.

 ## Tip 3: Trust, But Verify

When Darius reported that he had no homework, his parents wanted to trust him, but were wise enough to verify his claim. They did this in the following ways:

- School Website – This usually contained daily homework, but not all teachers were up-to-date all the time. After a few check-ins, they determined which teachers regularly posted and which did not. They compared the assignments written down in his planner to the teachers' posts.

- Homework Buddies – Darius was required to have a list of two responsible friends in each class he could call, when needed, to check on assignments. When the school's website wasn't enough, he was required to call one to verify there was indeed no homework.

- Teacher Initials – The easiest way to know if your child has work or not is to have the teacher initial his planner to verify the information recorded is correct. Some teachers are willing to do this, some are not. Explain the situation to your child's teacher to see if this is an option.

- Reward for Teacher Initials – Many teachers will not initial the planner unless the child seeks her out. This issue had been a problem for so long with Darius that I recommended they reward him for teacher initials. They had tried coaxing him into obtaining signatures in the past, but it rarely worked. He wouldn't remember to ask, and the teacher was often too busy at the end of the class to think about it. This time around, they agreed to give Darius 20 minutes of screen time for each teacher signature he obtained for his four main classes. So, he could earn up to an hour and 20 minutes of screen time by getting initials in each core subject – language arts, math, social studies, and science.

- Go High Tech – Students have many reasons for not recording assignments accurately. Some feel they can remember their work while others are just too preoccupied to take the time to write. Regardless of the reason, a voice recordable pen may just solve this dilemma. This gadget allows the student to record his homework without having to write it down. Prices range from the very basic with 20 seconds of audio time ($4.50 at www.amazon.com) to one with 1 GB of memory and 100 hours of audio. Priced at $99, the Smart Pen (www.livescribe.com) not only records the human voice, but also the written word. By tapping directly on paper, the audio can be replayed and notes can be saved to the computer. Disclosure may be an issue here – prior to recording anyone, make sure your child has a conversation with him or her.

Tip 4: Put It In Writing

Darius could be argumentative and oppositional at times, particularly when it came to homework. He was the type of kid who had to have a good reason to do something, especially when he disliked the task. He was a "what's in it for me?" student. Darius tended to respond well to a carrot, a motivator that made homework worth his while. When he knew both the upside and downside in advance, he was much more compliant. Knowing this about Darius, I suggested that his parents develop a brief homework agreement for him, enlisting his input. The written agreement would have to spell out exactly what Darius would earn for doing the two things his parents felt were imperative - writing down the correct assignments and completing the homework. It would also include consequences; however, I felt that Darius would respond far better to an accord heavy with rewards. They drafted the following agreement:

Homework Agreement

I, Darius Jones, together with my parents, agree to the following homework plan:

I agree to:

- Do a full 60 minutes of Designated Homework Time Monday-Thursday. If I don't have 60 minutes worth of homework, I will organize, read, or study.
- Show the completed work to an adult.
- Write down my homework assignments in math, science, social studies, and language arts. My parents can ask for verification at any time.

In exchange for the above, my parents agree to:

- Stop nagging me about my homework and only help if I ask.
- Let me hang out with my friends in the neighborhood until 7 pm. I can have friends over to play video games.
- Double my allowance at the end of the week if I follow these guidelines Monday-Thursday.

Signed_____Signed_____

The Problem

Anna – A 17-Year-Old Junior With No Way Out

Anna's elementary years were happy and academically successful, but it all came crashing down in middle school. Study skills did not come naturally to her and they weren't taught. Anna was simply not prepared to juggle seven classes, keep a tidy locker, and remember the right materials as she moved from class to class. Although her academic world was rocky, she enjoyed the social aspect of school. Friendships made school bearable.

Anna lamented, "In math class this year, I had to work harder than the other kids and force myself to pay attention in class, even when my mind drifted. It honestly wasn't easy. When I got home, I just couldn't remember how to do the homework problems. I hated math and math hated me."

The more I worked with Anna, I realized that her skill deficit in math was further impacted by poor organization and study skills. The combination of these factors made learning new material a real challenge. The further behind she got in math, the more she avoided it. By the start of high school, Anna's negative attitude in math spread quickly to the other subjects. Homework avoidance became her default mode.

Although Anna sees college in her future, she wonders if she'll ever make it out of high school. She has dug a hole so deep that she feels it's close to impossible to turn around her high school career.

The Solution

Tip 1: Tie Driving And Other Teen Privileges To Grades And Effort

The most important thing in Anna's life was her friends. She enjoyed navigating the social realm of high school. Anna was allowed to use the family car to drive herself to extra curricular activities during the week and to friends' houses on the weekends. The car equaled freedom to her. I suggested to Anna's parents that they tie car usage and evening plans to interim report card grades.

When I first met with Anna, she had just received her report card, and it wasn't what she and her parents had hoped. She earned a few Bs, many Cs, and a D in algebra. In the past, a yelling match would have ensued with Anna promising to do better next time. This time around, however, she was restricted from the use of the car on weekends and could only use it to drive back and forth to field hockey practice. She had to come straight home afterwards.

Anna's school year was based on the quarter system, with report cards distributed every nine weeks. Interim reports were sent home at the midpoint between report cards. A deal was struck between Anna and her parents. She had to demonstrate improved grades on the next interim (4 Bs and only 2 Cs in her five core classes - English, history, math, science, and French) in order to earn full driving rights.

This approach worked for Anna, but some kids respond better when incentives, such as driving or time with friends, are provided weekly or even daily. You can do this by tying the homework process, rather than long-term grades, to privileges. Acknowledging positive changes like more time spent on homework, beginning assignments on time, or evidence of test preparation can help to move your child in the right direction.

TIP 2: Stay With Sports

When I initially met with Anna's parents, they were ready to take her off the field hockey team, but I persuaded them not to do it. Anna loved the sport, obviously engaged in vigorous exercise (something that all kids need), and more importantly, was good at it. Anna needed something to bolster her self-esteem and this sport gave her the confidence she didn't gain from academics. It's been my experience that taking away too much does not change behavior or grades. So, if your first reaction is to withhold sports, you may want to search for other consequences that do not impact self-esteem.

 ## Tip 3: Consider A Study Group

For some students, small group learning is far more appealing and productive than going it alone. A carefully selected study group of your child's peers may help her get back on track. Positive peer influence has been well documented to improve academic success, and as an added bonus, study groups are fun. They promote learning, new friendships, and camaraderie. Group discussion can be a better means of studying than reading or reviewing alone. William Glasser, author of *Schools without Failure*, said,

"We Learn...
10% of what we read
20% of what we hear
30% of what we see
70% of what we discuss
95% of what we teach others."

Anna loved the idea of a study group, and when her parents suggested she choose two friends in her physics class to come over to prepare for the upcoming exam, she contacted them immediately. If you think a study group may be just the ticket to get your child learning, go ahead and suggest it, but lay the ground rules first. Rules should include:

- A start and end time.
- A quiet place to meet, but one that is within earshot.
- What they will be covering during the session (an agenda isn't necessary, but the students should have a general idea of how and what they will study).

 ## Tip 4: Get A Tutor – And Fast

Anna's parents were wise enough to realize that Anna needed a tutor to teach her the skills she didn't come by naturally. They hired a tutor to help her with better homework habits, study skills, and math content. They knew that at the age of 17, Anna wouldn't be able to accept their help. The combination of tutoring and limiting driving privileges turned Anna's grades and self-confidence around.

Students that avoid need immediate intervention. If you've tried many of the ideas presented in this chapter and found that there are too many emotions involved in homework discussions, it's time to seek a neutral third party. Get started now by hiring a professional who specializes in helping struggling learners.

The key to making this work is the right tutor/student relationship. Disheartened students, especially teenagers, are very personality-sensitive. If they do not gel with the person you hire, all bets for success are off. In managing my tutoring agency, I've spoken with thousands of parents. After I've taken the time to listen to their fears and needs, I always ask, "Tell me about the type of person you think your child would like," and "What kinds of teachers has he connected with in the past?" Invite the child to participate in the process as well. Get her perception of the problem, and more importantly, the type of tutor with whom she would enjoy working.

Tip 5: Seek Professional Help To Evaluate The Problem

Avoidance can be a manifestation of other underlying problems. If your child has been struggling with homework for a long period of time or you see a sudden drop off in his performance, consider other professional help in addition to tutoring. Even if his avoidance is a result of perfectionism, getting outside assistance will shine a new light on the problem and provide fresh approaches. You may want to consider these two options:

Obtain an Evaluation – Testing by a licensed professional can uncover learning, attention, or emotional difficulties that may negatively impact your child. The results may provide a diagnosis that will entitle him to extra help at school. Begin by speaking to your pediatrician about your concerns and ask for a referral for psychological/educational testing. Scheduling testing and waiting for the results and a written report take time. Be sure a tutor is in place in the interim.

Counseling – Parent, family, and/or individual counseling, may be an important part of understanding why life is so difficult for your child. It will also give you strategies for dealing with tough situations.

Chapter 7
Homework Made Simple
Checklist

The Avoider's habits can be changed with simple, proactive strategies. Have you:

- ✓ Given back some control to your child by allowing choices?

- ✓ Established Designated Homework Time?

- ✓ Trusted your child, but verified that homework is complete?

- ✓ Tied teen privileges, such as driving, to grades?

- ✓ Encouraged a study group?

- ✓ Sought outside assistance if needed?

Chapter 8

What To Do About
The Inattentive

Goals

In this chapter you will learn to help your Inattentive child by:

- Using fidget toys, background music, and games.

- Encouraging self-monitoring techniques.

- Rewarding him with Mystery Motivators.

- Chunking homework into shorter sessions to increase focus.

- Communicating with teachers to develop a school program.

Some parents spend an inordinate amount of time getting their child to do two things – focus and finish. Every parent can relate to the problem of focusing well enough to stay on task and finishing the assignment at hand. Homework that should take 45 minutes ends up consuming two hours. To deal with this dawdling, parents try cajoling, handholding, badgering, and walking away in frustration. When that fails, the encounter escalates to threats and yelling. A battle ensues and there is no clear winner. As it turns out, there are better ways.

Does This Sound Familiar?

Test It Out!	A Usually	B Sometimes	C Rarely
My child takes an inordinate amount of time to complete homework.			
My child needs redirection to get homework done.			
My relationship with my child is affected because I nag him to finish homework.			
Even after I reprimand him for not paying attention, the unwanted behavior returns quickly.			
My child is easily distracted by others in the room and outside noises.			
The teacher tells me that my child is missing out on learning because of problems paying attention in class.			
I think my child would do so much better if he could focus.			
My child is bright in many ways, but the final work product doesn't reflect true intelligence.			

Total number of checks in each column	A	B	C

If you answered "usually" or "sometimes" to most of these questions, then this chapter is for you.

Is There Really A Problem?

For many students, inattention is a real problem with serious negative consequences, yet this is not the case with all students who seem preoccupied. Some students who appear to be distracted actually attend quite well. Psychologist Jackie Andrade of the University of Plymouth in England found that the act of doodling while listening to others actually improved recall, even when the students appeared not to be paying attention. Participants in the study not only remembered 29 percent more information than the non-doodlers, but they also took notes more accurately.

Although other research has found that multitasking and daydreaming can be distracting, don't assume that your child's tendencies are always counter-productive. The next time you see him off task, ask a few general questions related to what he's studying. If he's able to answer them, his distractibility may not be impacting learning. If, however, this is not the case, read on for simple solutions for the distractible/inattentive student.

Why He Can't Pay Attention

Most kids want to get homework done and out of the way just as much as their parents want them to. The problem is that they may not have enough internal self-control to get the job done. Contrary to how it may seem, children are not deliberately inattentive. In all my years of teaching and tutoring, I never met a child who enjoyed being pestered, yelled at, or teased because he couldn't pay attention.

Some distractibility and inattentiveness is merely due to age. Young children do not yet have the capacity to focus for extended periods of time. Some may simply be very active and need a chance to release pent-up energy, while others may have ADHD (Attention Deficit/Hyperactivity Disorder).

Students who have difficulty focusing may present differently, hence, the solutions to helping them with homework vary. On one hand, you have students who are highly energetic, fidgety, and just cannot sit still. These hyperactive kids seem like they have a motor inside of them. They're constantly looking around and getting out of their seat. On the other hand, you have those who daydream, stare into space, and work slowly. In fact, their inattention in class may go unnoticed because they are so well behaved. Some children present qualities of both – hyper-activity and inattention. In one homework session, they can go from being fidgety to daydreaming; this is not unusual. They may not con-sistently have the mental energy or concentration to maintain focus.

Recognize The Consistently Inconsistent Pattern

I recently consulted with parents who felt their child simply did not care about school. They believed that if their daughter really focused, she could complete her homework on time, every day. They thought this was true because she had actually done it a few times. That's what is frustrating about kids who struggle to focus – they are consistently inconsistent. Some days they toil like a well-oiled machine. Other days they are like an old out-of-sync grandfather clock. It's easy to assume that if a child has a good day, she can produce the same strong, con-sistent effort day in and day out, but this typically isn't the case. Chil-dren with attention difficulties want to sustain focus, but no matter how hard they try, they cannot always do so. Punishing inattentive behavior doesn't work. Positive reinforcement and a few creative ideas do work.

A Word About Medication

Some students who fit the profile of the Inattentive student may also meet the criteria for a diagnosis of ADHD. Once identified, families face a difficult dilemma - treat ADHD with medication or try to get along without it. Some students who take medication find that it begins to taper off around the dinner hour. Scheduling homework for an earlier time, right after school, tends to provide students with a large enough window to complete assignments before the medication wears off. If this is not the case, be sure to discuss the problem of homework time and the issue of medication wear-off with your child's treating physician. There are new, longer-acting formulations that effectively increase attention and decrease distractibility for 10 to 12 hours with one dose.

This chapter will provide you with field-tested tips that are easy to implement. These strategies are designed for all kids who are inattentive, hyperactive, or both, whether or not they have a formal diagnosis.

HELP IS ON THE WAY!
TOOLS FOR THE INATTENTIVE

The Problem

Stephen – A Fourth Grader Struggling To Focus

Stephen was an adorable fourth grader who loved science and nature. His parents came to see me because they were worried that Stephen's well-documented issues with attention were causing real problems in the classroom. I observed his class one morning and arrived just before the students did. Stephen entered the room, seemingly ready for learning, but in a short time he was in another world. His teacher reminded him several times to complete his morning work.

Problem cont.

She said, "Stephen, you've got to get that worksheet done before you switch classes." He nodded, furrowed his brow and got started again, intent on completing the assignment. Within five minutes, a classmate diverted his attention and the cycle of frequent distraction and teacher redirection began anew.

The other kids in the class snickered behind his back. His mother, Nicole, was deeply concerned not only about his academic performance, but also about his lack of friends. She said, "He'd rather spend two hours glued to the video game joystick than playing with a friend." That was only the tip of the iceberg – homework was taking three times as long as it should have. Nicole observed many of the same off-task behaviors at home that concerned his teachers in the classroom. Her constant redirection to keep Stephen on task was wearing on her and him. Nicole wondered how Stephen would ever get through the elementary years, much less middle and high school.

Like many students, Stephen struggled with inattentiveness at school and at home. He was a daydreamer, seemingly in another world and lost in his own thoughts. Nicole needed help on both fronts, but we decided to start by making changes at home.

The Solution

 ### Tip 1: Set Up A Study Space

The first step I suggested was easy to implement, but it took some de-tective work up front. Most Inattentive students need a fairly quiet place to study, but a small group of these students thrive on the hum of a busy area. Last week, I ran into a friend at a local coffee shop. She had her laptop out, folders stacked, and Blackberry in hand. Her mini-office was primed for a day's work. I thought this was strange knowing she worked out of her home, so I asked if she was waiting for a colleague. She replied, "No, I just can't focus with all that quiet. I get more done here." This friend is an adult version of so many students who struggle with attention. In setting up a study area for your child, do some experimenting.

- For two days, have your child do his homework in a well-traveled area and then switch to a quieter area for the next two days. Which is best for him?

- If you determine your child does better in a quiet place, find an area free from household action, but close enough to monitor his activity. The dining room often works well.

In Stephen's case, he actually did much better in a quiet place away from distractions. Because his parents had a small home office, they carved out a niche for Stephen and this became his special homework space. Here are some other tips you may wish to consider when setting up a study area for your child.

- For highly Inattentive kids, a desk in their room is usually not practical. There are too many diversions.

- Be sure the TV and cell phone are off and the student does not have internet access to surf the web.

- For some, sitting at a traditional desk isn't productive; however, there are other options. One is an exercise ball chair (www.sitin-comfort.com) which is a sturdy exercise ball in a steel frame with a comfortable back rest. This alternative has become so popular that teachers are using ball chairs in their classrooms instead of conventional chairs.

- Another option is a lap desk (www.roomitup.com) — a mini-desk that lies across your child's lap. The top contains a flat writing surface and the underside is a beanbag cushion. With a lap desk, the student can sit on the couch or another chair more comfortably.

- Still others need to stand, pace, or even lay on the floor. Some children actually perform better doing their homework standing up. Their ability to recall information for a test is enhanced when they walk around, reciting definitions to themselves.

Think outside the box – movement stimulates focus and makes homework a lot more fun. I once worked with a high school student who studied for tests as he rode an exercise bicycle and a younger girl who learned her multiplication facts while jumping rope!

For more information on setting up a study space in your home, see pages 66 and 67.

 ## Tip 2: Make A Mountain A Molehill

Depending on the age of your child, he may only be able to focus well for 20 minutes at a time.   Often, the time you spend refocusing his efforts after 20 minutes may be better spent giving him a break so he can recharge and begin again. This can be done in two ways – by task or time.

By task – Make a lengthy assignment seem shorter by:

- Folding a worksheet in half. Instruct your child to do the top half, show it to you, and then finish the second half.

- Allowing him to choose the problems or questions he wants to do first. When he's done with half of them, go on to the rest.

- If the assignment is in a textbook, use Post-it arrows to show the starting and stopping points. Give a short break upon completion.

By length of time – Inattentive students can usually focus and attend to detail for short bursts. Try one of the following techniques:

- Set the timer for 5, 10, or 15 minutes. Tell your child, "Work as hard as you can for this time. When the timer goes off, you can daydream or play for 5 minutes."

- Set the timer for a length of time for which you absolutely know he'll be successful. When he succeeds, lengthen the span by a minute.

Tip 3: Support Self-Monitoring

In the past, Nicole had been overly involved in her son's homework. Her constant redirection put too much of the onus on her and not enough on Stephen. In essence, his schoolwork had become hers.

With homework, a parent's goal should be to teach some basic strategies, monitor the child's progress, and let him go at it alone. The "alone" part is what many parents hope for, but it can feel impossible for those with children who require a great deal of oversight and handholding. Instead of the burden falling on you, teach your child to self-monitor so that he can operate more independently. Sometimes, though, in order to help your child gain independence, you may have to think creatively and try something a little bit unusual.

I suggested that Nicole consider purchasing a WatchMinder (www. watchminder.com) to aid Stephen's self-awareness. This novel watch can be programmed for reminders at any time of the day (take medication, feed the dog, leave for lacrosse, etc.) but the best feature is a re-occurring vibrating alarm. It can be set in four to ten minute intervals, depending on the child's age. The silent alarm is a cue to your child that he should be working on homework. Every time he feels the vibrations, he's to record his progress. Is he on or off task? The WatchMinder is an excellent tool to promote self-awareness. By adding a form to record on task behavior, you can set up a component to provide rewards if he is consistently on task.

My Self-Monitoring Form

Check Yes or No when the watch vibrates. Check Yes if you are sitting at the table doing homework, mark NO if you are out of your seat or daydreaming.

Yes	No

If I earn 7 out of 10 checks, I may have
30 minutes of free time.

Tip 4: Communicate With Teachers To Coordinate A School Program

Because Stephen needed additional support in the classroom, I suggested that Nicole work with the school to obtain formal accommodations. Students with a diagnosed disorder that impacts their performance may be entitled to classroom accommodations or special education services. Because Stephen was diagnosed with having ADHD, Nicole was able to obtain a 504 Plan, a document that mandates classroom accommodations to meet the needs of a child with a disability.

Whether or not your child needs formal assistance, keeping the lines of communication open with the classroom teacher is incredibly important. The recommendations I gave to Nicole can work for your child, too.

Create a Cuing System

You may want to suggest that the teacher create a special nonverbal cue that means, "Listen – this is important," or "Get started on your work." Ideas include tapping her shoulder, touching her elbow, or rubbing her hands together once eye contact is made. This quiet signal is far better than verbal reprimands because the student isn't singled out. At home, you can use the same nonverbal cue.

If it's difficult to get a student's attention, a single word can be used that says, "Look at me." Since this was such a problem for Stephen, Nicole and his teacher chose the word "umbrella." When Stephen heard the word, he was to look at the teacher and listen for any directions that might follow. It worked beautifully and Stephen was not singled out. As a matter of fact, the teacher reported that the whole class was paying better attention to her when she called out, "Umbrella!"

Negotiate the Unfinished Schoolwork Dilemma

When schoolwork goes unfinished, some students are kept in from recess or lunch or burdened with these assignments at night in addition to homework. Sit down with the teacher and strategize ways to get all this work done in school. Adding schoolwork on top of already assigned homework can demoralize a student and create a downward spiral at home.

Keep a Homework Log

Every child encounters difficulties with homework from time to time. If this seems to be the rule rather than the exception, it is important to document how much time is being spent on homework. Teachers may be unaware that homework is so problematic because they only see the final, corrected product, not the inordinate amount of effort behind it. Try this:

- Create a form similar to the one that follows.

- For at least one week, preferably two, jot down the date and length of homework. You may also want to document any reasons you see for your child's homework struggles.

- Meet with the teacher and share the information you've recorded. If the documentation reveals your child is spending too much time on homework, a reduction in work load may be necessary. Be sure to word your concerns in a non-threatening manner. Consider saying "Mary is having a tough time with homework. I've been keeping a homework log. Do you have any suggestions to help us?"

Date	Assignment	Time to Complete	Issues
Jan. 5	Wordly Wise	50 minutes	Trouble looking back at passage to find answers
Jan. 5	Science essay	1 hour	Couldn't get ideas onto paper
Jan. 6	Book report rough draft	90 minutes	Same as above

The Problem

Mackenzie – An Energetic Third Grader

At the age of three, Mackenzie's parents noticed that she had a lot more energy than the other kids in the neighborhood. She was always on the go, hardly ever running out of steam. Family and friends referred to her as "spirited," "precocious," and "a ball of fire."

I began working with Mackenzie's family when she was nine years old and in the third grade. Even her brash nature that seemed entertaining when she was younger, wasn't cute now. Schoolwork proved difficult for Mackenzie although she was more than capable. She'd start a task, but would quickly move on to something more interesting before completing it. Her work piled up; one worksheet after another was left undone. Mackenzie was floundering because her distractibility and inattention were making her unavailable for learning.

Problem cont.

Homework was much the same. Her mother said that it was like "pulling teeth" to get her to focus. Her parents reported that she was a constant fidgeter – when she wasn't twirling her hair, she was usually swaying from side-to-side in her seat, or tapping her fingernails on the table. The only solution her parents found was to sit right next to her; otherwise the 45 minutes of expected homework time turned into two hours. Mackenzie's mother asked, "Why can't she just sit at the table and get it done like her sister?" Homework was creating a rift in their relationship, and Mackenzie was only nine years old.

The Solution

 ### Tip 1: Let Her Fidget

As a young teacher, I always had a few students in my class who cared more about playing with the pencils and erasers in their desk than focusing on me. When they weren't fiddling with objects, they were rocking in their chairs or getting out of their seats. My first inclination was to take away the objects that distracted them. I soon realized that eliminating these distractions didn't make it any easier for these students to pay attention.

In fact, the traditional notion that people need complete silence and a sterile environment in order to concentrate has recently come under fire. Various studies have shown that distractible students can actually attend better when they are given something to hold or touch. If you find that your child tends to fidget by touching objects around her, tapping her feet, or rocking in her chair, it's likely that she's craving sensory input. Many children, like Mackenzie, need this type of stimulation, especially when tasks are tedious or boring. The solution is to allow your child to fidget in a way that doesn't distract other siblings or classmates. Here are a few suggestions that worked for Mackenzie and can be effective for your child, too.

- A recent study by Suneeta Kercood published in the *Journal of Behavioral Education* found that a plastic, twistable toy called the Tangle Jr. (www.tanglecreations.com) significantly improved students' abilities to stay on task and answer a greater number of math problems correctly. By simply manipulating this toy in their hands, fourth grade students were better able to focus. The Tangle Jr. makes no noise; therefore it won't bother other children sitting nearby.

- Wikki Stix (www.wikkistix.com) and good old-fashioned stress balls work in much the same way. They help to keep the brain engaged and the student on task. Keep these items in the study area just like typical school supplies.

- One of my favorite ideas is to create a texture strip by cutting a three to four inch section of double sided tape and adhering felt to the back of it. Have your child stick it to the underside of his desk. Experiment with different types of felt textures such as smooth, rough, and fringed. Texture strips give kids immediate sensory input through their fingertips. This strip is especially effective for kids who needed a blanket or soft toy to play with in order to fall asleep as toddlers.

- Amazingly, chewing gum activates the brain. You won't find many kids who will resist this focus-enhancing intervention! In fact, many schools are realizing the benefits of gum and are now allowing it in the classroom.

- Weighted lap pads (www.flaghouse.com) provide pressure that helps with sustaining concentration. To use this quick fix, place the pad over your child's lap while he's sitting down working on homework. For some students, lap pads provide a feeling of calmness, allowing for longer stretches of attention.

- Read *Fidget to Focus* by Roland Rotz and Sarah Wright to get more ideas on fidgeting to pay attention.

After utilizing some of these strategies, Mackenzie's parents saw marked improvement, and more importantly, Mackenzie enjoyed using the tools. The parents encouraged their daughter to use these strategies (her favorite was the Tangle Jr.), but did not demand it. They merely made sure the fidget tools were in her study area when she began homework.

 ## Tip 2: Insist On Exercise – The Miracle Drug

Dr. John Ratey, author of *Spark: The Revolutionary New Science of Exercise and the Brain* states that aerobic exercise "almost immediately elevates dopamine and norepinephrine and keeps them up for a period of time a little bit like Ritalin or other medications used to treat ADHD. It also helps to still impulsivity and works to wake up the executive function of the brain. Exercise improves the learners. Their senses are heightened, their focus and mood are improved, they're less fidgety and tense, and they feel more motivated and invigorated." Given the incredible benefits of exercise, it made sense for Mackenzie's parents to:

- Encourage her to exercise before homework was even started. They found that when they promoted vigorous outside activity like taking the dog for a run, going for a bike ride, or even good old-fashioned outdoor free play, Mackenzie was focused and in better spirits at homework time.

- Give her breaks between assignments with the option of going outside or running a bit on the treadmill. Even though breaks were meant to be short, they can still be long enough to get the heart pumping.

- Allow her to complete homework after soccer practice. Mackenzie loved soccer more than anything else, but it was tough for her to finish all of her homework before leaving for practice. Her parents discovered that doing half the work after practice was more productive and less stressful because she was more alert and focused.

Tip 3: New Ways To Teach Boring Facts

Nearly all students are focused and engaged in learning when the instruction is stimulating, fun, and interactive. Because distracted students reach a saturation point much faster than others, making rote learning more appealing will allow for prolonged attention. Try the following novel approaches to help your child memorize.

Games For Math

Games offer an excellent alternative to traditional flash cards for teaching math facts.

- Use any board game, such as Checkers or Operation. Before each player takes his turn by selecting a game card or rolling the dice, he must first pick up a flashcard (no answer visible) and state the answer. If the answer is correct, he can then choose a game card/roll the dice and play the board game as usual. For more on incorporating games, be sure to read the next chapter. Kids love this approach because it makes something that was once painful, painless.

- Toss an inflatable Multiplication Quiz Cube (carsondellosa.com) back and forth to practice facts. Make up rules such as, "Catch it and say the fact your left thumb is touching." My students are keen on this game because it gets them moving around.

- Grab a deck of cards and play Multiplication War. Each player flips up two cards from their deck, multiplies the two numbers together and states the product. Whoever has the highest answer wins all four cards. The person with the most cards at the end of the game wins.

- Make up rhymes for facts that are the most difficult to learn. The 6, 7, and 8 tables are often tougher than the rest, so put those facts to a rhyme. For example, "Pizza, pizza at my door, 8 times 8 is 64!"

If you insist upon using flashcards, let your child hold the cards and quiz you. Studies show that merely allowing the student to hold the cards and take on the role of the teacher increases time on task and retention of data.

Spelling Words

Most kids are better at writing their words when practicing for tests than saying them out loud "spelling bee" style.

- Because color helps to focus attention, encourage your child to highlight the silent letters or irregular patterns in words. This simple technique aids visual memory so that children are able to picture the word in their mind as they write it.

- Trace, Copy, and Recall - Fold a piece of notebook paper into thirds. Have your child trace a list of words into the first panel. The child then copies the traced words into the second panel. Finally, the night before the spelling test, use the third column for a practice spelling exam.

- Rainbow Writing is a fun way to use color, especially for those who are visual learners. The student chooses three bright colored pencils. He writes the word once in the darkest color and then traces over it twice, each time with a different colored pencil.

- For more active students, you can play catch to teach spelling! Throw the ball to your child while saying the first letter of the word. When your child throws the ball back, he should say the second letter. Keep going until you reach the end of the word!

- If your child is more of a "listener," have him tape record himself saying the word, spelling the word, and saying the word again. As he learns, have him recite along with the recording.

Vocabulary

Try these interactive approaches to help your child learn new vocabulary words.

- Board games can be used in lots of ways. Instead of a deck of flashcards, substitute word cards. As a player picks up a word card, she must state the definition correctly. If her answer is correct, she may then choose a game card. If her answer is not correct, take those word cards and put them off to the side in a separate pile. After the game is over, review those incorrect terms with her until they become automatic.

- Put words and definitions on separate index cards. Spread the cards out face down, now play the traditional matching game by choosing two cards. The goal is to obtain a match by selecting the correct term and its definition.

- When assisting with memorization, focus on the facts or words that your child does not know. This will cut down on time spent on homework. Don't be afraid to change your approach when you see that the novelty is wearing off. I often use a game for a few weeks and then put it on the back burner until a later date. Newness and excitement enhance learning, retention of information, and make homework fun again!

 ## Tip 4: Try Mystery Motivators

Mystery Motivators are incentive systems designed to randomly reward positive behavior. Research supporting this technique indicates rewards are effective when granted in a manner that the student can't predict. Here's how it works:

1. With your child, target one to three behaviors such as finishing homework on time, recording all schoolwork legibly in the planner, or adhering to Dedicated Homework Time. Write goals down and post them in a conspicuous place.

2. Now, create a list of six to eight motivators. This will only work if the reward is of interest to the child. For some kids it is extra screen time, for others it's a chance to order pizza for dinner. My children love to be driven to school so they don't have to wake up so early to catch the bus.

3. Write each motivator onto a slip of paper. Then, add the same amount of blank slips to the stack. Now you will have at least six motivators and six blank slips. Fold each one in half, hiding the words. Place into a paper bag or hat.

4. On a daily basis, determine if the goal was met. If it was, have your child pick from the slips in the bag. He has a 50/50 chance of choosing a motivator. When a winning slip isn't selected, remind your child that he will have a chance on another day. Just like the TV show *Wheel of Fortune*-every spin isn't a winner.

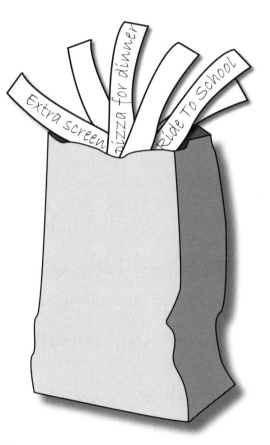

With any reward program, you'll need to change the prizes every so often. As excitement decreases, it may be time to conjure up new motivators.

This may sound like a lot of effort, but kids of all ages love it! Once Mystery Motivators is set up, it's easy to maintain. Add to the fun by providing a bonus, such as two selections from the bag, if goals are met Monday through Friday. You can find colorful Mystery Motivator kits on the web at www.reallygoodstuff.com.

The Problem

Samir - A 7th Grader
Who Just Can't Get It Done

I first met Walid at a parent presentation I gave at a local middle school. He shared that his son, Samir, was getting disappointing grades partly because he couldn't get his homework done. One night their intense argument ended with Walid hurling insults that he couldn't believe came out of his mouth. He knew that things had to change, but wasn't sure how to proceed.

When it came to homework, Samir's obstacle wasn't getting started, it was finishing. He would routinely begin an assignment, but become so distracted that it usually wasn't completed. In addition, Samir dawdled well into the evening with very minimal pay off. He seemed to be doing hours of homework, but had little finished work to show for his efforts.

The Solution

 ## Tip 1: Create A Break Menu

Samir's distractibility was exacerbated by the fact that there were too many interesting diversions available to him. He had free access to his laptop and phone, all in the comfort of his own room. I suggested that Samir's study area be moved to a common area on the first floor of the house. Even though he was in seventh grade, he wasn't ready to work completely alone.

Samir was the type of student who responded well to rewards, so together, he and I created a "break menu." The menu, written on a 3x5 card, consisted of a list of small rewards he chose from after he finished an assignment. It was clear that Samir became so drawn into everything electronic, that anything with a screen couldn't be part of the menu. We replaced these distractions with activities similar to those below. For example, after he completed his math homework, he could shoot hoops in the driveway.

Good Break Menu Ideas	Probably Not So Good
• Playing with the cat	• Playing video games
• Shooting a few hoops	• Watching TV
• Getting a snack	• Using the computer
• Building with Legos	• Texting
• Making a quick phone call	• Going to a friend's house

It turned out that Samir did not need time restrictions on his breaks, as he typically got back to work, but many children do. If your child has a tendency to prolong breaks, put a time limit on them. A 10 minute break is typically adequate, but every child is different. Whatever time frame you determine is best, have your child set the timer. When it goes off, the break is over. By simply changing Samir's homework location and allowing him to choose small rewards after each assignment, he was able to focus significantly better.

Another variation of this strategy is a *Break Log*, a more structured approach to scheduling breaks. With this method, the student writes down the amount of time he can realistically focus on any given assignment. The next step is to jot down the way in which he will reward himself upon completion.

In Samir's break log, he agreed to work diligently on his history essay for 20 minutes before taking a break. He knew this was attainable, but that he'd likely struggle with longer bouts of time. He set his watch timer for 20 minutes. When the time was up, he took his well-earned break. If he wasn't finished with the assignment at that point, he would continue if he was close to completing it. If Samir was too far from the end, he'd take his break and then finish the rest before going on to the next assignment.

BREAK REWARD LOG		
Subject	Time	Reward
History essay	20	Take dog for a walk
Math	15	Start making Christmas list
Science poster	30	Call Jordan about weekend movie

Samir eventually only needed to use this approach with work that he found to be "way too boring." He was able to sustain focus in subjects that he liked, but still needed to use a timer and break log with homework he felt was tedious.

Tip 2: Allow Background Music

One battle that Samir insisted on winning had to do with music. His father feared it was a likely distraction, but Samir felt otherwise. He said he needed it to focus. Samir may hold the winning hand in this debate. A growing body of evidence supports his view. The use of background music is correlated with positive attitudes toward learning. Many students perceive music as enhancing their ability to perform paper and pencil tasks. What's more, they rated television as having a negative effect on their learning.

In a study of fifth grade science classes, researchers determined that there was a significant increase in on-task performance when instrumental music was played in the background. The positive effect was far greater in boys than girls mainly due to the fact that fewer girls exhibited off-task behavior in the first place.

Additional studies suggest that only certain types of music are beneficial. Instrumental music, especially non-percussion, slow to medium paced pieces, help by increasing attention. That means that if students are focused on reciting the lyrics, their focus is on the song, not on homework. If you want to incorporate music into your child's homework routine, try the following:

- Agree to allow instrumental music. Provide your child with a couple of CDs or ideas of songs he can download.

- Setup an iPod with speakers or CD player to use for background music during homework time. Be sure this iPod includes home-work-friendly music.

- Consider making your child's personal iPod off limits during homework. It's too hard to monitor.

Tip 3: Use A Mirror To Improve Concentration

Samir and his father were grateful for the positive changes that were taking place during homework time, but they looked at me strangely when I advised using a mirror to help with focus. I explained that research demonstrates that a mirror placed in the homework area helps kids to stay on task.

In studies by Dr. Sydney Zentall, students who actively looked in a mirror placed in front of them performed better on academic tasks than those who did not use a mirror. Why? The mirror served as an attention monitor in a way. When students looked into the mirror and realized they were daydreaming, they quickly returned to the work in front of them. Not only do mirrors improve attention, the study found that they help students to be more accurate in their answers. By placing a self-standing mirror in your child's homework area and encouraging him to use it correctly, you'll help to improve his attention and independence.

Chapter 8
Homework Made Simple
Checklist

The Inattentive student's habits can be changed with some basic strategies. Have you:

✓ Set up a study space based on the way your child focuses best?

✓ Utilized fidget tools to increase attention?

✓ Allowed background music?

✓ Incorporated exercise into the homework routine?

✓ Taught your child to break down lengthy assignments by time or task?

✓ Encouraged the use of self-monitoring techniques?

Chapter 9

What To Do About The Easily Frustrated

Goals

In this chapter you will learn how to help your Easily Frustrated child by:

- Avoiding power struggles.

- Dealing with difficult behaviors that create family conflict.

- Designing checklists and token economy reward programs.

- Breaking down tough assignments that create frustration.

- Encouraging resilient behavior.

- Using games to change a negative mindset.

Some kids are naturally easy-going, compliant, and adaptable. With very little input from you, they come home from school, sit right down, and do their homework. If they encounter a problem they can't solve, or read a passage they don't understand, they're able to ask for help.

Other kids are not as even-keeled. Their moods are quick to change, their tempers are volatile, and they are easily frustrated. They often complain that their homework is too hard or too boring. If they encounter difficulties before you have a chance to intervene, they have a meltdown. Their low frustration tolerance makes homework a battleground.

Does This Sound Familiar?

Test It Out!	A Usually	B Sometimes	C Rarely
My child is obstinate and moody, but also highly entertaining when in the right frame of mind.			
There are days when homework results in tears and tantrums.			
My child complains that work is too hard or overwhelming.			
She becomes upset with a sudden change in plans or schedule.			
My child struggles to bounce back from negative experiences.			
Power struggles occur in my home.			
My child's emotional state prevents her from completing tasks and/or assignments.			
My child shuts down at the first hint a task will be difficult.			
Sometimes work is hastily completed because she is too upset to do a good job.			

Total number of checks in each column	A	B	C

If you answered "usually" or "sometimes" to most of these questions, then this chapter is for you.

Holds It Together In School

Easily Frustrated children do whatever it takes to hold everything together during the school day. Their behavior in school is generally appropriate, leading parents to ask teachers, "Are you sure you're describing my child?" The difference between the home and the classroom is that the classroom is inherently structured; routines and expectations are typically the same, day in and day out. In addition, kids don't want to appear different from their peers, so they are more likely to adhere to behavioral norms. When they get home, they're exhausted from performing academically and conforming to classroom expectations, so they unleash their frustrations on their parents. Because they feel safe at home, they don't put as much effort into acting appropriately as they do while in school. This results in an explosion of pent-up emotion that is targeted towards those who love and care for them most—their parents or caregivers.

The Problem With Production

Parents are the first to witness emotional flare-ups when the going gets tough. An assignment that may be easy for other students often requires extra mental effort for Easily Frustrated students because they're slow to process the information or their anxieties impede learning. Despite average or high intelligence, some have trouble writing down their answers as fast as they can think of them. Frustration grows when they can't keep up with the pace of the class or homework. Many have difficulty in production, which means that they understand the concept, but just can't get it down on paper efficiently. It's easy to understand why school can be so difficult for these children.

Emotionally Charged Academics

While most children feel a sense of accomplishment when they have successfully tackled a tough assignment, these students rarely derive pleasure or satisfaction from completion. Easily Frustrated students also have the uncanny ability to drag their parents into nightly arguments over seemingly basic assignments. If asked to correct answers, they become upset. Most children have the capacity to accept feedback, make necessary changes and move on, but these kids are easily derailed.

Once they are off the track, it is not easy. Instead of the parent assisting with homework content alone, he now has to manage his child's negative feelings associated with past failures. His role as a parent may extend to that of a counselor and tutor, even though he may be ill-prepared. Parents are between a rock and a hard place in these situations because the child may view their help as punitive, even though she still needs some direction. If the cycle isn't broken early on, the battles continue into adolescence.

Nature vs. Nurture

Are these behaviors due to biological disposition, accumulated academic difficulties, or choices in parenting? Could it be that a past history of struggles combined with lack of resiliency creates a perfect storm? Over the years, the pendulum has swung back and forth on the answers to these questions. Child development experts now recognize that biology plays a big part in personality traits. Some children are easy-going and resilient by nature while others are certainly more challenging to raise. Dr. Sonja Lyubomirsky's 2007 research demonstrated that there is a direct correlation between happiness and resiliency, which is a key characteristic that Easily Frustrated students also lack. She found that 50 percent of happiness comes from a person's genes and 10 percent is due to life circumstance, such as income, health, or marital status. A whopping 40 percent of these factors are malleable, meaning they can change over time with the right influences.

Factors That Determine Our Happiness

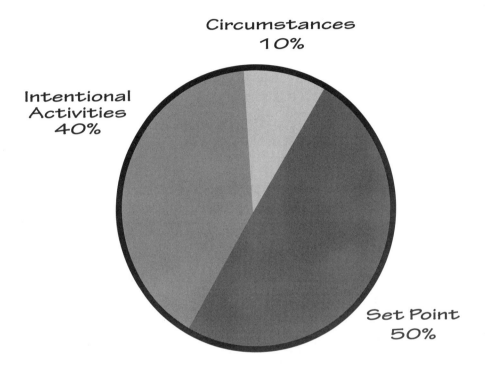

Circumstances
10%

Intentional
Activities
40%

Set Point
50%

Source: Lyubomirsky, 2007, *The How of Happiness*

In parenting a less resilient child, it's important to focus on this 40% that can be changed, not on the 50% that cannot.

HELP IS ON THE WAY!
TOOLS FOR THE EASILY FRUSTRATED

The Problem

Gabrielle – A Feisty Fifth Grader

Gabrielle exhibits all of the traits of a child with low frustration tolerance. Her parents, Patti and Joe, struggle to cope with their daughter's emotional volatility and are at their wits' end about how to deal with homework strife. Conflict now dominates their relationship.

Gabrielle is quick to anger and often gives up on tasks out of frustration. When assignments are short and straightforward, she does well. However, when her teacher assigns work that seems overwhelming, such as a book report or story writing, Gabrielle shuts down. Homework drags on for hours. There's lots of yelling and all too frequent emotional meltdowns.

Gabrielle's fifth grade teachers seem surprised when her parents share their struggles at home. Although the teachers see that Gabrielle is easily discouraged in class, they have never experienced the meltdowns her parents encounter. Joseph and Patti wonder how their daughter can be so different in school. They need strategies to help Gabrielle overcome her frustrations so that homework can be completed with less stress.

The Solution

 ## Tip 1: Reverse The "To Do" List

Gabrielle may be similar to the child in your home right now. These students often require different parenting strategies from their easier siblings to help them move past their current educational roadblocks.

Many students, especially those who procrastinate, do better when they begin with a challenging assignment. By doing so, they get this assignment out of the way early on instead of putting it off until late in the evening. However, the reverse is true for the Easily Frustrated student. When your child is ready to begin homework, encourage her to number the assignments in the order in which they'll be completed - #1 should be the assignment she perceives to be the easiest or the most enjoyable. For example, if your mathematically-inclined child comes home with spelling, math, and reading homework, allow her to do math first. Gabrielle's parents were amazed to find that this simple strategy put her in the right frame of mind to tackle harder subjects.

If your young child does not yet have a planner, ask her to lay the assignments on the table; arrange them in order - first, second, third, etc., with the most difficult work saved for the end. Place sticky notes on each assignment indicating the chosen order (1st, 2nd, 3rd, etc.).

 ## Tip 2: Break It Down

Help your child break work down into manageable chunks you know he can accomplish. If he's successful doing the first task, he's more likely to attempt the next one. This strategy quells frustration before it rises. Try the following:

- Use Post-it arrow flags. Place one at the starting point and another part way through the assignment, Say, "All you have to do is start here and end there. Come and show me your work when you're done." Visual learners especially like this approach.

- Help your child to get started. Observe her completing the first item so that you are sure she can do it accurately and independently. Then, set the timer for five to fifteen minutes. Encourage her to work as hard as she can during that brief time to get over the hump.

- Color code the symbols in math (red for addition, blue for subtraction, green for division, etc.). Encourage her to do the "green" problems first or give a choice of order.

- Cover the bottom portion of the worksheet or put an index card over the more difficult problems. Suggest that she complete only the visible part first.

- Ask for her input by saying, "How can you chunk this assignment into two parts?" Advise that she do the first part, take a five minute break, and then finish the last section.

Ultimately, you'll want your child to internalize these strategies and use them on her own. At first, you'll need to model these techniques, but soon your child will be able to do them independently. Be sure that the materials are readily available in her study area. When most kids see Post-it arrows, highlighters, and timers in front of them, they are visually reminded without you having to say anything.

 ## Tip 3: Talk So She'll Listen

Gabrielle's parents reported that life became far less dramatic after they established daily routines and helped her break down seemingly insurmountable assignments. The one thing that they had a hard time changing was their daughter's mood. They finally realized this was not in their power, but it was often possible to change her reaction by choosing the right words. Let your child know that you understand that homework isn't always easy. You don't have to modify your expectations, but identifying with her struggle will make her feel heard.

Your Child Says	Instead Of	You Respond With
"This is a stupid assignment!"	"I agree! What is that teacher thinking?"	"Why do you think it's stupid? What do you think is the teacher's rationale behind assigning it?"
"Mrs. Baker is so unfair. I can't believe she's making us write an entire essay!"	"She obviously has a reason. That's why she's the teacher. Now get to work."	"Mrs. Baker wants you to become a good writer. This type of assignment will help you practice writing a topic statement and supporting ideas."
"I CAN'T DO THIS. IT'S TOO HARD!"	"Yes, you can do it! It's not too hard. You did this type of problem yesterday."	"I know this worksheet is hard for you. Math is a tough subject. Let's try the first couple of problems."
"I'll never learn this. I don't care if I fail the test."	"You better not fail that test, Buddy. If you get below a C on your report card, you're grounded."	"Let's take a look at what's causing the problem. Can you show me what you need to study?"

In addition to empathizing with your child, reinforce toughing it out. Praise him the moment you see him persevere through a difficult homework assignment. Always take the opportunity to notice the positive behavior if you want it to be repeated. In Gabrielle's case:

Situation: Math has given Gabrielle nothing but headaches this year. She refuses to "show her work" but, today for some reason, she solved the first problem using a step-by-step approach.

Parental Acknowledgement: Patti could say, "Gabrielle, the steps you've written down are excellent. That effort will really make a difference in getting the correct final answer. Way to go!"

Situation: Gabrielle has struggled in her first year of Spanish. She does the bare minimum to get by, but tonight she asks her dad to help her study for an upcoming quiz.

Parental Acknowledgement: Joseph could respond: "I'd be happy to help you study for your quiz. Has your teacher taught you a specific way to remember this information or do you want to make up your own study method? I bet this preparation will help you feel a lot more confident tomorrow."

Furthermore, emphasizing effort over achievement can make a huge difference in academic performance. Harold Stevenson, a professor at the University of Michigan, found that one main reason Asian students outperform American students is their parents' emphasis on perseverance. They stress effort – "Work as hard as you can, and you will be successful" - over intelligence. Next time, instead of saying, "What did you get on that test?" or "You're so smart, I know you can do this," say, "How long did you study?" or "With a little extra practice, you'll get the hang of it!"

The Problem

Peter – An Eighth Grader
Engaged In Power Struggles

Peter was the third and youngest child in his family. According to his dad, Sam, the two older children did their homework after school without prompting. Peter, on the other hand, watched TV or played video games when he should have been doing schoolwork. Sam recounted a recent evening when he discovered Peter watching TV even though his English homework was not completed. Sam erupted and grounded Peter for an entire month. He felt badly for overreacting, so he reneged on the punishment.

Sam asked me to make a home visit to help the family implement some basic homework strategies. As I entered the house, I heard an argument evolve. Sam said, "Peter, come on, you've got to study for that geography test. You got a D on the last one." Peter resisted, "Dad, what's the point? I don't see why I need to know that stuff. It's stupid!" Sam countered, "Don't be ridiculous. You're just looking for excuses. If you spent half the time on your schoolwork as you spend on TV, we wouldn't be having this conversation." Then Peter rolled his eyes and yelled, "Whatever!" Frustrations and tempers escalated until Peter stormed out of the room.

Sam realized homework was seriously affecting their relationship. He knew that he was too easily drawn into verbal sparring matches with Peter. Sam also understood that schoolwork was more difficult for Peter than it was for his other sons. Peter was easily discouraged even when it was clear he was capable of doing the work. When this occurred, he looked for any way out, which usually included sitting in front of the mind-numbing television.

The Solution

 ## Tip 1: Post Homework Rules

Part of the problem in Sam's household was that there were no written expectations. Although this was not an issue for his older children, Peter needed clear rules so that he knew what was expected of him. Sam needed to put daily routines and requests in writing. You may find this is the case with your child too. Without such policies, emotionally charged kids will push their parents' buttons. However, if you establish a clear set of homework policies and unambiguous consequences, then you're able to remove emotion from the situation. When your child ignores the rules you've set down, the consequences are clear. I encouraged Sam to develop policies with his son, so they sat down one evening and agreed on the following:

Homework Policies

- *TV goes on only after homework is done and shown to a parent.*
- *All assignments must be complete by 8 pm.*
- *Homework must be put into binder. Binder goes into backpack.*

Rewards for Completing Homework

- *One hour of screen time, to start after 7 pm.*
- *Choice of screen time – TV, computer, video games, cell phone.*

Consequence for Not Following the Rules

- *Loss of screen time for the evening. One warning will always be given before a consequence.*

When creating policies for your household, be sure to engage your child. Ask for his input so that he feels he's a part of the decision making process. Your child will be more responsive if he feels included.

 ## Tip 2: Ignore The Little Things

When two people are engaged in a power struggle, there is never a winner. Before you start to travel down that road, consider ignoring annoying, but minor behavior such as:

- An exasperated sigh (it's better than an expletive).

- Rolling of the eyes (just turn away).

- A comment like "fine!" after you have asked him to get started on homework.

Although it's tempting to say, "Don't you roll your eyes at me!" or "What did you say?" remember to:

Focus on the big picture, not the details. For example, if you want your child to complete his science project, don't insist that he correct one or two misspelled words. The goal is to simply get it done. Keep the big picture in mind and ignore the little things that may not matter a month from now.

Keep comments short and non-judgmental. It's a habit to pontificate but, 99 percent of the time, kids have tuned out. Not only do words go in one ear and out the other, they often don't even go in. If your child chooses to argue with you, calmly repeat your request and then walk away.

Tip 3: Take A Break From Power Struggles

What should you do when you realize that a disagreement is becoming a power struggle? Extricate yourself ASAP by taking a quick break. Use these words:

"Let's take a 15 minute break. I'll be back at 2:34 pm."
Be specific about time.

"We're not agreeing on this assignment. Let's both think of one solution and meet back at the table after dinner."

"We're both upset. Let's grab a quick snack and then talk about a compromise."

"Can we reach a compromise here? Let's talk about ideas when I get back from walking the dog."

The Problem

Anya – An Emotional Third Grader

Anya Park was a glass half empty type of kid. She found the downside to most anything related to learning. School hadn't been easy for Anya. She was slow to read in first grade and had to work harder than her peers to keep up. During the school day, she put forth the best effort she could, but became moody and pessimistic when homework time rolled around.

Her parents were loving and warm, but at times, Anya tested their patience. When she arrived home from school, she whined about starting her homework. It seemed like it took her a half an hour just to retrieve the assignments from her backpack. When Anya finally put pencil to paper, she'd complain that the work was too hard.

Problem cont.

There were days when she became so upset that she'd put her head on the table and refuse to go any further. Her behavior made her typically easy-going parents aggravated and upset. They tried changing her mood, but that rarely worked. So just to keep the peace, they would allow her to put away her homework until later that evening or even finish in the morning.

No day was ever the same. Some days, they could get Anya through her work without tears, but other days, she required intense coaxing. Mr. and Mrs. Park realized that they needed to get off the after-school roller coaster and deal with their daughter's frustrations with homework.

The Solution

 ### Tip 1: Use A Homework Checklist

The difficulties Anya's parents encountered were partly due to a lack of routine, rewards, and consequences. I suggested that they create a checklist that specified what Anya needed to do after school in order to complete homework.

You too can create and maintain a checklist for your child similar to the one that follows. First, think about what you want your child to do after school and narrow the list down to two to four homework-related tasks. Now, determine what it will take to motivate your child. Anya loved playing an internet game called Club Penguin, so for her, it was screen time.

> **In order to establish a true reward, the incentive cannot be available at any other time during the day.**

In the past, Anya's parents allowed her to have computer access at most any time, so there was never any incentive for her to complete the work.

Finally, record any other rules below the checklist. In Anya's case, she was given two reminders to finish her work. Her mother, Jackie, had asked Anya, "How many reminders do you think you'll need?" Anya stated that she'd need three prompts.

You can come up with your own ideas, but remember, that once your child earns the reward, you cannot take it away. For example, if she earns 30 minutes of screen time, but then hits her sister, I don't recommend taking the earned privilege away. Instead, consider another consequence such as time out. Children are more likely to follow through with incentive programs if they know their "winnings" won't be withheld.

Frequently, younger students enjoy earning something tangible, not just a checkmark. In addition to placing a check by each accomplished task, students can earn a token (marble, penny, ticket, etc.) which is then placed in a jar. In addition to daily privileges, accumulated tokens can be traded in for larger rewards. For example:

Reward	Cost
Having a friend sleep over	25 tokens
Chore pass	10 tokens
Later bedtime	30 tokens
Additional allowance	50 tokens
Movie with a friend	20 tokens
Toy under $10	40 tokens

Anya's Homework Checklist

WHAT I HAVE TO DO	MINUTES I CAN EARN	Did I Earn Points?				
		☺ Mon	☺ Tues	☺ Wed	☺ Thurs	☺ Fri (opt.)
Layout HW on dining room table when I get home.	10 min	✓	✓			
Do my HW on my own.	10 min	✓	✓	✓		
Show mom my completed HW.	10 min		✓	✓		
Put my HW in the folder in my backpack.	10 min	✓	✓	✓		

- If needed, I can take a 5 minute break between assignments.

- Mom can give me two reminders or else I lose my minutes of screen time for that "to do" task.

- My earned time starts 7 pm. If I do not turn off the screen by 7:40, I will lose 10 minutes the following day.

Signed by ___Anya___ and ___*Jackie*___

 ## Tip 2: Role-Play

Sometimes children don't seem to learn from their mistakes. Even when there are consequences in place, they still repeat the same negative behavior patterns. They understand what they shouldn't do, but don't know how to replace that behavior with a different one. Role-playing can demonstrate this in an effective way. It takes the emotion out of the situation and injects some humor into the process of changing behavior. Before beginning homework, role-play a difficult situation that has caused problems in the past.

Say This	Do This
"I know that this math can be tough sometimes. Let's practice what you can do instead of getting frustrated and pounding the table. Watch - I'll be you."	*Pretend to be your child. Clench your fists and yell in frustration about math. Kids often find this funny and realize just how their behaviors seem to others.*
"Now you tell me what I can do instead of clenching my fists and yelling." Brainstorm with your child appropriate responses.	*Make a list of three alternatives. These might include:* • *Take five deep breaths.* • *Go to the refrigerator and get a drink.* • *Put the math (or whatever assignment is causing distress) away for now and start the assignment you like best.* • *Take a break by listening to music for ten minutes.*

Practice with your child at least a couple of times. In the future, when you see behavior escalating, remind her of one alternative. If she's unable to choose a better solution, practice again. Change takes time and you'll need to revisit role-playing down the line to make sure it sticks.

Tip 3: Use Games To Change A Negative Mindset

Unfortunately, there is a small group of students for whom learning is miserable, regardless of the amount of parental encouragement. In order to make it through school intact, these kids must begin to gain a small amount of pleasure through academics. By associating homework and learning with satisfaction and fun, they're more likely to overcome a negative mindset. This transformation can be accomplished by making learning enjoyable by using games. It's easy to reinvent the good old fashioned board games you played as a kid by simply adding a deck of homemade 3x5 index cards. Here's how:

Academic Subject	Games	How to Play
Math facts or studying for math test	Sorry! Candy Land Chutes and Ladders	Write facts or practice problems on blank cards. Player picks a card from the deck, and solves the problem. If he's correct, he can take his turn on the board game.
Spelling	Connect Four Battleship Operation	Write spelling words on blank cards. Player picks a card and says the word out loud. The other person spells the word. If he's correct, he can take his turn.
Reading	Hungry Hippos	Read a page from a text book or novel and reward with a game of Hungry Hippos.

Games aren't just for young kids. Middle and high school students also enjoy this novel way of reviewing material or preparing for a test. One of my favorite ways to make learning come alive is by putting a new spin on the classic game, Jeopardy! Take four envelopes and label them 100, 200, 300, and 400. These will hold the review questions that can be found on a teacher-provided study guide. If your child didn't receive one from his teacher, brainstorm with him questions that might be asked on the test. Next, cut out the questions from the study guide into strips and place them into the envelopes (100 being the easiest level). Take turns choosing, reciting, and answering the questions until the envelopes are emptied and one "contestant" is crowned the winner. This will likely be your child since the material is most familiar to him!

Don't be shy about incorporating games into studying with your older student. Not only is this method much more fun than traditional means, but it's also multi-sensory. Students are learning through three important senses – auditory, visual, and tactile – which makes information more likely to stick.

Tip 4: Create A Family Mantra

Finally, a "never give up" motto helps unite families, not just the child experiencing difficulty. Repeat the phrase in the face of a difficult situation and encourage your child to do the same. If you haven't already, brainstorm a mantra like:

"The Park family never gives up."

"When the going gets tough, the Parks get going."

"In the Park family, we always finish what we start."

"Try, try, and try again, and then you will win!"

Chapter 9
Homework Made Simple
Checklist

Your Easily Frustrated child's habits can be changed with some easy-to-implement and maintain strategies. Have you:

✓ *Reversed the To-Do list?*

✓ *Helped your child break down large assignments into manageable chunks?*

✓ *Remained calm and ignored minor off-putting behaviors?*

✓ *Created a homework checklist or family homework policies?*

✓ *Taken a break instead of becoming part of a power struggle?*

✓ *Introduced games to make learning enjoyable?*

✓ *Created a family mantra?*

Part III

Troubleshooting: From Study Skills To Sticky Situations

As you've seen, the recipe for classroom and homework success requires much more than innate intelligence. It must include the right blend of priorities, parental involvement, and student responsibility. But sometimes, even when all the ingredients are carefully mixed, the end result isn't what you thought it would be. If you've followed the suggestions in this book but still feel a vital ingredient is missing, take time to read the next two chapters.

So often, one of the missing ingredients is adequate study skills. In chapter 10 you will learn about four must-have techniques for reading comprehension, note-taking, memorization, and planning ahead. These are skills that all kids need to succeed in school. They are vital during the elementary, middle, and high school years, but more importantly, they help students in college and in their working careers.

In addition, the following chapter will help your child to identify his learning style. Kids like knowing how they learn best and this information will help them to choose the correct strategies for their strongest learning mode.

Despite your best intentions, your child may resist your help or present you with other obstacles. Chapter 11 targets difficult situations and the solutions that will allow you to overcome even the toughest circumstances. From the challenges of dealing with testy teens, divorce, or lying, unique situations will be covered. This information may be the final garnish for serving up academic success and family harmony.

Chapter 10
Improving Study Skills

Goals

In this chapter you will learn how to help your child improve study skills in order to:

- Increase reading comprehension by using active reading strategies.

- Take simple and easy two and three-column notes from text and lectures.

- Improve memorization and recall of important facts.

- Plan ahead and prepare independently for upcoming exams.

- Identify his or her learning style and use it to improve test scores and grades.

After watching countless students struggle over the years, it has become clear to me that the ability to study effectively separates well-prepared from ill-prepared students. Some students are very motivated, but have inefficient study skills. They spend hours preparing for exams only to earn an average grade. Others lack the motivation to put forth enough time and effort into studying.

Study Skills - The Missing Curriculum

In recent years, standardized testing has become a prominent fixture in American classrooms. Teachers no longer have the time to teach study skills, nor do they always have the training to do so. The majority of students acquire good study habits through the snippets they get in the classroom, from their parents, and most typically through trial and error. They know what works for them and they apply those strategies. But for many students, appropriate study skills are not easily attained. They need direct instruction in HOW to study.

Even when classroom instructors teach bits and pieces of study methods here and there, students are not learning to apply these powerful, proven methods routinely. In this chapter you will learn about the effectiveness of mnemonic devices – a truly superior memory technique. Students may learn to utilize mnemonics once or twice during the school year, but without enough practice they never learn to make routine use of it.

The great news is that parents don't have to be professional educators to help their children learn basic study skills. The following five top study skills are easy to teach and incredibly effective to help students master content and build confidence.

How Can I Help My Child With Reading Comprehension?

Active reading strategies are some of the best techniques to help students improve comprehension. When young children read aloud, hearing their voice helps to keep them alert and tuned in to the story. However, as students age they begin to read silently and, for some students, herein lies the problem. While reading silently, they become passive learners. This means that they read the words without truly grasping or retaining the information.

How many times have you been reading a book, found yourself at the bottom of the page, and then realized that you had no idea what you had just read? This happens to all of us, especially when our minds are elsewhere. But this happens so often to some students that it feels normal. Active readers are cognizant of the fact that important information was missed, so they go back to the top of the page and reread, while passive readers keep on going. By the end of the passage or chapter they have little comprehension. These students must develop active reading strategies; after all, learning is not a spectator sport.

The three main techniques outlined here help passive readers become active ones. Encourage your child to try them all to see which works best for him or select one that feels most comfortable.

Active Reading Strategy #1
Elicit Background Knowledge

Prior to delving into the first sentence, competent readers think about connections they already have to the text. If the title is "Patrick Henry," the reader may pause for a few seconds to think, "Who was Patrick Henry?" or "What do I already know about him?" Your child can activate background knowledge with these techniques:

The Z-Sweep – Performing a Z-Sweep can help students get the gist of what lies ahead. Instruct your child to move his hand from the left to the right under the first line, then back around through the body of the text, and then finish with a sweep from left to right at the bottom. He should read the first sentence, glance or sweep through the body, and then read the last one or two sentences. By using this strategy, he can gain a cross-section of what he's about to read - an instant comprehension booster.

The Z-Sweep is a simple, yet powerful strategy for short stories or passages when used correctly. Remember, it is a pre-reading strategy, not a speed reading technique. The Z-Sweep allows students to get a general idea of the material before they read for detail.

The Z-Sweep

Patrick Henry

Patrick Henry was born in Hanover County, Virginia, on May 29, 1736. Although he had little formal schooling, Henry's father was a well educated man and worked hard to educate his son. Over the years, Henry tried his hand at farming and running a store but found success in the study and practice of law. He became well-known for his eloquence and intelligence and soon found himself a revered public speaker with a growing pool of supporters. This helped to fuel his move to politics and Henry's conviction only grew with his success. Although he was a member of the House of Burgesses, Patrick Henry supported the rights of colonists and believed the colonies should have the ability to govern themselves.

Henry served as the first and sixth post-colonial Governor of Virginia; first from 1776 to 1779 and then from 1784 to 1786. He is well-known for his famous speech "Give me Liberty, or give me Death!" and is remembered as one of the Founding Fathers of the United States of America as well as a radical and influential advocate of the American Revolution. He stood for republicanism and denounced corruption in government officials during his time. After the Revolution, Henry fought alongside other anti-federalists in opposition of the replacement of the Articles of Confederation with the US Constitution because they feared the constitution would weaken many of the individual freedoms that were gained from the war.

Although the Constitution was ratified in Virginia despite his protests, Henry was instrumental in the passing of the Bill of Rights in 1788. He died June 6, 1799 in his home in Virginia but remains a prominent figure in US Colonial history.

SCAN and RUN – The SCAN and RUN strategy, developed by George Salembier in 1999, has been found to significantly improve reading comprehension in middle and high school students. Unlike the Z-Sweep, SCAN and RUN can be used for longer sections in textbooks. To simplify this method, students should focus on the first half of the strategy—the SCAN.

Before reading:

S = Survey Headings and Turn Them into Questions
Find each bold heading, and turn it into a question. For example, if the bold heading is The Trojan War, the student should think, "What happened in the Trojan War?"

C = Capture the Captions and Visuals
Glance at the pictures or diagrams and read each caption.

A = Attack Boldface Words
Now, focus on the terms in bold. Quickly read these words for an understanding of the main vocabulary words.

N = Note and Read the Chapter Questions
This is perhaps the most important pre-reading strategy. Read the review questions at the end of the section first. This will help with main idea comprehension.

While reading:

R = Read and Adjust Speed

U = Use Word Identification Skills

N = Notice and Check Parts You Don't Understand and Reread

Active Reading Strategy #2
Make Margin Notes

Margin notes are summary phrases the student jots down in the margin of a book as he reads. This strategy forces the student to engage in what educators call "self-talk," a technique in which the learner questions himself about what he's reading. You can coach your child to use this strategy by saying, "After you read a page in your novel (or a section in your textbook), ask yourself, 'What did I just read?' or 'What is the main idea here?' " His answers should be briefly recorded in the page margin. This simple task improves comprehension because the student must summarize the information he's just read. Reiterating and condensing text is one of the best ways to understand and remember. It will also make studying much easier because the main points are now recorded in the margins. If writing in the textbook is not an option, your child can use Post-it notes.

Active Reading Strategy #3
Use Selective Highlighting

Over the years, I've met many kids to whom I've given the official diagnosis of "highlighter happy." These students take a great strategy and use it incorrectly by highlighting as they read. By the end of the page, practically every sentence is marked. Instead, teach your child to read first and then go back to selectively highlight only the essential/important terms, phrases, or dates. Studies have shown that students are better able to retain information that is color coded. But the color of the highlighter is not important (although most favor yellow or pink); it comes down to personal preference.

Consider purchasing highlighting tape when marking in the school-issued text isn't an option. Removable colored tape can be purchased at www.reallygoodstuff.com. Now, in order to prepare for an upcoming test, your child can review what's been "highlighted" with tape and remove it as he masters the materials.

Highlighting and Margin Notes

One of the most famous events in early Greek history is the Trojan War. The war is well-known for its length, legendary players, and the Trojan horse, but many may not be familiar with the reason for its inception. Steeped in Greek Mythology, the Trojan War is said to have begun at the wedding of Peleus, the King of Thessaly, and Thetis, a sea nymph. The wedding celebration was held in Troy and almost all the gods and goddesses were in attendance. One goddess, however, had been left off the guest list. Eris, goddess of discord, was not invited due to her penchant for causing conflict wherever she went.

War started at wedding

Eris wanted revenge and decided to start a fight at the wedding. She marked an apple "for the most beautiful" and tossed it into the middle of the banquet hall where all the gods and goddesses were celebrating the marriage of Peleus and Thetis. Once the goddesses spotted the apple, they began to quarrel over which one of them should possess it and hold the title of most beautiful. After much argument, they narrowed it down to Hera, Athena, and Aphrodite. Paris, the prince of Troy, was said to be a good judge of beauty and was given the job of choosing the winner. Each goddess fervently tried to bribe Paris in order to win the golden apple.

Eris not invited, revenge

Threw "most beautiful" apple.

Hera promised Paris land and kingdoms. Athena promised him victory in war and everlasting fame. Aphrodite offered Paris the mortal Helen, daughter of Zeus, in order to persuade Paris to give her the golden apple and the title of most beautiful. Paris could not refuse her offer. He was anxious to claim Helen and set upon his journey to Sparta.

Paris chose Aphrodite b/c she promised Helen

Helen was already married to the King Menelaus of Sparta but Paris stayed with Helen and her husband as a guest. When Paris left Sparta, he outraged the King by taking Helen with him. The King gathered his army and set out to declare war on Troy to reclaim his wife from Paris.

War started!

Trojan War:
  -Started @ wedding of Peleus + Thetis
  -Goddess Eris not invited, annoyed, started trouble
  -Threw apple "for most beautiful" goddess fight
  -Troy's prince, Paris has to decide & goddess Aphrodite wins by
   promising him Helen
  -Helen's married to Menelaus & war starts over Helen-Sparta vs. Troy

What Is The Best Way To Take Notes?

Being a good note taker is absolutely essential to academic success. The columned note-taking strategies are easy to use for recording information from textbooks or lectures. The beauty of this method is that once it is implemented, studying for exams becomes a cinch.

Two-Column Notes

To set up columned notes the student divides or folds the paper into two sections, labeling the left one-third "key words" and the right two-thirds "notes." On the left the student records the main idea, and on the right he jots down an explanation using short phrases. This system works particularly well when taking notes from a textbook.

This note taking method helps kids to be more independent learners. Your child can fold his paper vertically on the line between the keywords and notes so that he can quiz himself and not rely on someone else to assist with studying. With only the left column visible, he asks himself, "Who was Paris?" and then says the answer. He checks his reply by flipping over the page. He continues to review in this manner, repeating and retesting himself on the terms he cannot automatically recall.

Three-Column Notes

Three-column notes are highly effective for younger students and visual or tactile learners. In addition to the first two-columns, a third section for a drawing is added. By drawing a picture of the concept or term, children are hooking a concrete visual image to the information they need to remember.

Example of Two-Column Notes

Key Words in Trojan War	
⬭ **Key Words**	**Notes**
Paris	- Prince of Troy, son of King Priam - Judged beauty contest - Chose Aphrodite - Won Helen of Sparta
⬭ Eris	- Goddess of discord - Not invited to wedding of Peleus + Thetis - Started fight amongst goddesses by throwing apple for the prettiest
Helen ⬭	- Wife of Menelaus, Sparta - Promised to Paris - Brought to Troy by Paris - Fought over in Trojan War

Example of Three-Column Notes

Key Words in Trojan War		
Key Words	**Notes**	**Pictures**
⭕ Paris	- Prince of Troy, son of King Priam - Judged beauty contest - Chose Aphrodite - Won Helen of Sparta	
⭕ Eris	- Goddess of discord - Not invited to wedding of Peleus + Thetis - Started fight amongst goddesses by throwing apple for the prettiest	
⭕ Helen	- Wife of Menelaus, Sparta - Promised to Paris - Brought to Troy by Paris - Fought over in Trojan War	

Most students are under the impression that "less is more" when note-taking. While being succinct is important, the fact is that the more notes students take, the more information they will be able to recall later. In this particular case, "more is more!" Students do need to avoid taking notes verbatim from the teacher, though. Instead, using abbreviations, paraphrasing, and summarizing will help improve recall later on.

How Can I Help My Child Remember and Retain?

In classrooms across America, teachers strive to provide engaging lessons, meaningful homework, and assessments, but more often than not, our students aren't LEARNING HOW TO LEARN. Kids walk out of their classrooms armed with study guides, notes, and chapters to read, but they don't know how to put that information into storage for retrieval tomorrow, next week, and three months from now.

The master memory methods found in this chapter link what the student already knows to new information. Encourage your child to try all of the following or choose one based on preference.

Master Method #1 - Mnemonics

Researchers have found that using mnemonic devices can help students improve their memory skills by connecting to-be-learned information to what the learner already knows. Do you remember learning the order of operations in your beginning algebra class? I bet you can still recall, "Please Excuse My Dear Aunt Sally," a mnemonic device for:

P-Parenthesis

E-Exponents

M-Multiplication

D-Division

A-Addition

S-Subtraction

It's likely that PEMDAS was the only way you could recall the order of operations. Trying to do so without this memory strategy would have been difficult. Another common mnemonic device is HOMES, which is an acronym for the Great Lakes – Huron, Ontario, Michigan, Erie, and Superior. This strategy is flexible; it can be used with virtually any type of rote memorization. Once kids are shown how to use this technique, they come up with all kinds of catchy acronyms to make retention easier.

Master Method #2 – Smart Card

Just as drawing a picture in the final column of three-column notes helps a student anchor and retrieve information by enlisting sensory memories, adding an illustration and personal sentence to an index card with the term on one side and a definition on the other creates an interactive "smart card". First, let's look at how to create the cards, and then we'll examine the key learning concepts.

Creating a Smart Card

On the blank side of an index card, the student writes the vocabulary word or concept.

Term | Definition, Visual, Sentence

On the other side, he does three things:

1. At the top of the card he writes a definition or brief explanation of the term.

2. In the middle of the card, he writes one sentence that shows how the term relates to him personally.

3. At the bottom of the card, he draws a diagram or picture.

Why are the drawings and personal sentences a key element? When the learner sees or hears the word "docile," he creates a mental image of the dog in his mind's eye, triggering a connection to his personal sentence. Instead of rotely memorizing a term and its definition, the student has created a meaningful way to ensure retrieval.

Master Method #3 - Sleep On It

Believe it or not, studies show that students who go to bed right after studying retain more information than those who engage in activities such as listening to music, watching TV, or playing video games. Sleep somehow solidifies the learned material, whereas other activities may interrupt the brain's ability to process and store information. Encourage your child to keep test material by his bedside to review just before going to sleep.

Research also supports the notion of adequate sleep for optimal learning. A study recently published in the journal, *Learning and Memory*, found that students are likely better off spending their time catching some Zs instead of cramming, studying into the wee hours of the morning. Although an increasing number of high school students are reporting they "pull all-nighters" before a big test or exam, this is not an effective strategy.

How Can I Help My Child Plan and Study?

Practice makes permanent when studying for tests. When information has been recalled often, its representation in the brain is reinforced, making memory stronger- just like exercising a muscle. First and foremost, this exercising involves planning. Just as you wouldn't try to drop 10 pounds in just two days for your high school reunion, your child cannot cram for a final exam in an unreasonable amount of time either.

Prior planning: There is no way around hard work and planning ahead. Once a deadline for a test is given by the teacher, it should be recorded in the planner along with the specific study goals leading up to the final date. This simple strategy is explained on page 127 and I encourage you to reread it if studying for tests is tough for your child.

Now, let's go back to examine the powerful use of column notes. Once the student records notes from lectures or text, he's not done. That evening or prior to the exam, he must quiz himself. This skill is essential because it does not involve you, the parent. Initially teach him how to fold the paper vertically, read the word in the left column, ask himself the meaning, and finally, flip the paper to check his response on the right side. This practice is golden for helping students to independently prepare for tests.

Pull out those Smart Cards as well. Rehearsing over and over again until material is over-learned transfers what is in short-term memory to long-term. The student must practice until he's able to say the word and then use the picture cue to automatically recall the information on the card.

All too often kids are quick to throw up their arms in defeat. "I studied for two hours for that test. How did I get a D? It's not fair!" It's been my experience that their "studying" is very passive. Visually scanning each page of the text book is not studying! Actively taking notes to review, quizzing oneself, or creating and solving possible test questions IS studying.

Make a Practice Test: Long-term memory is enhanced when students take "interactive" practice tests. A highly effective way to prepare for an exam involves creating a practice test. This means that the student generates a sample test of questions he thinks may possibly be on the exam. This information can come from old tests and quizzes, a study guide, or notes. I always encourage my students to ask their teacher about the format of the test. Will it be comprised of essay questions, fill-in-the-blank, or multiple-choice? Having this information helps with preparation.

Furthermore, this method is perfect for studying for math. I once had a student who said to me, "With math, you either know it or you don't. You can't study for a math test." His reasoning was sadly incorrect. Students can study for math tests; the best way to prepare is to jot down example problems from the book or prior homework problems that are correct. The student can then solve them, one by one, referring back to the correct steps if he can't recall the solution.

A Note About Test Anxiety

Students are quick to complain about test anxiety. Although some may be accurate in their self-diagnosis, others are nervous because they haven't prepared properly. Perhaps they've read their notes, skimmed the chapter, and reviewed the study guide, but that is not true preparation. Quizzing oneself until the information is committed to memory is imperative. If an answer is "on the tip of his tongue," it's likely that it wasn't stored into memory effectively and more work is needed.

Why Is Learning Style So Important?

Most people have a preferred way to learn. Some learn best by listening, some have to observe every step, while others have to do it to learn it. The fact is that individuals need all three modalities to truly commit information to memory: visual, auditory, and kinesthetic. While students are typically stronger in one area than another, the trick is figuring out the preferred modality and capitalizing on strengths. Encourage your child to take a few minutes to complete this informal inventory. Try it out yourself, too! The answers may surprise you.

Learning Styles Self-Assessment

1. **In order to memorize information, such as the spelling of a difficult word or locker combination, you:**

    a. Practice over and over again.

    b. Recite the word or numbers out loud.

    c. Visualize the word or numbers in your head.

2. **When you want to learn new song lyrics, you:**

   a. Dance around and play air guitar to the beat.
   b. Sing along to the radio.
   c. Download the lyrics and read them.

3. **While you study, you like to:**

   a. Walk around and review your notes.
   b. Discuss the material with your parents
   or friends.
   c. Read your notes or textbook independently.

4. **When preparing to go somewhere new, you prefer to:**

   a. Walk, drive, or bike the route ahead of time.
   b. Listen to someone tell you how to get there.
   c. Look at a map.

5. **When you get a new gadget that needs to be assembled, you:**

   a. Just start putting it together.
   b. Ask someone to read you the directions.
   c. Read all of the steps before you begin.

6. **If you have to work on a project with others, you would rather:**

   a. Help to build and construct a model.
   b. Participate in group
   discussions and brainstorm ideas.
   c. Draw graphs or scribe group notes.

7. **You tend to like classes that include:**

  a. Hands-on experiments.

  b. Lots of lectures.

  c. Reading assignments.

8. **When reading a textbook that you're not particularly interested in, you:**

  a. Squeeze a stress ball or move around to make yourself more comfortable.

  b. Would like to follow along while listening to it on tape.

  c. Have to take notes and highlight information.

9. **When studying a play in English class, you prefer to:**

  a. Act it out.

  b. Listen to the play read by others.

  c. Read the play silently to yourself.

10. **When you are able to choose a project and present it to your class, you would rather:**

  a. Create a working replica.

  b. Give a presentation.

  c. Create a poster.

11. **When you are distracted, you most often find yourself:**

  a. Fidgeting or playing with your pencil.

  b. Listening to or participating in conversations.

  c. Doodling on your notebook paper.

12. When you work at solving a challenging problem, do you:

    a. Make a model of the problem or walk through all of the steps in your mind?

    b. Call a few friends or talk to an expert for advice?

    c. Create a list of the steps you need to take and check them off as they're done?

Once you have finished your inventory, add up the number of a's, b's, and c's. Tally up your answers and "Voilà!" you have a snapshot of how you learn best!

If you answered mostly "a,"	you are primarily a kinesthetic learner!
If you answered mostly "b,"	you are primarily an auditory learner!
If you answered mostly "c,"	you are primarily a visual learner!

Totals a: _____ b: _____ c: _____

Once your child understands his or her learning style, this information can be used to their advantage for studying.

Auditory learners learn best by listening. Your child may want to:

1. Practice out loud.

Have your child practice reading notes, chapters, or other material out loud. This will increase both his comprehension and retention of new information.

2. Form study groups.

By studying in a small group, your child will be able to aurally process the information heard during discussions and one-to-one interaction. The auditory reinforcement will support your child in absorbing information that he may otherwise miss just by reading.

3. Take a lot of notes.

Auditory learners become so engrossed in discussions that note-taking is an afterthought. Even though your child may have excellent recall of lectures, he should absolutely take notes. Having notes serves as a back up for the details that may be forgotten after class. Furthermore, encourage him to review the notes within 24 hours as this helps with retention.

A Note About Doodling

Many auditory learners tend to doodle during lectures much to their teacher's chagrin. However, this is not so bad! Recent studies have shown that students who doodle actually pay attention better than those who do not.

Visual learners learn best by observation. Your child may want to:

1. Focus on pictures.

Visual learners should focus on diagrams and pictures in their text books. Some students are tempted to skip these items, but they will readily absorb the material this way.

2. Use three, instead of two-column notes.

Visual learners specifically benefit from the use of the three-column note method described previously in this chapter. The addition of a picture provides another way for students to remember and recall information much more efficiently.

3. Try multiple colors.

Visual learners can use multiple colors for either note-taking or highlighting. For instance, green can be used for main ideas and yellow can be used for supporting details. Another way to use color is by type of information. For example, people's names can be highlighted in blue, vocabulary in orange, and events in pink.

4. Use graphic organizers.

Since visual learners process information through sight, graphic organizers are the quintessential way for these students to break down and synthesize materials. Students can use Venn diagrams to compare and contrast two concepts or webs to outline and brainstorm for essays. Visit the website www.graphicorganizers.com.

Kinesthetic learners are "hands-on" types, they learn best by doing. Your child may want to:

1. Get up and move.

To memorize, students should feel free to pace or walk around while reciting important information or using flashcards. If this is not possible, they can use fidget toys like stress balls, texture strips, or other items discussed on pages 175 and 176. Similarly, lying on the floor, sitting in a bean bag chair, or doing homework while rolling on an exercise ball will help kinesthetic learners satisfy their need for activity in a less distracting way.

2. Get engaged in the text.

Simply listening to a lecture or reading a book will not commit information to memory. Kinesthetic learners have to utilize active reading strategies or they will remember little of what they read. Columned notes are also a must.

3. Take the role of the teacher.

When reviewing material for an upcoming test or merely doing practice homework problems, ask your child to show you how it's done. Give him the opportunity to take control and be the teacher. Not only will he get the opportunity to review, but he'll have a better attitude doing it. The best way to learn something is to teach it to others.

4. Have fun with interactive games.

Peers or parents can work with kinesthetic learners by tossing a ball while reciting facts (vocabulary, states and capitals, or really anything), playing hangman to study spelling words, or a quick game of Jeopardy to prepare for a test.

"I hear and I forget, I see and I remember, I do and I understand." Chinese proverb

Chapter 11

Handling Difficult Situations

Goals

In this chapter you will learn:

- How to help teens who resist adult support.
- How working parents with limited time can monitor homework.
- How divorced parents can consistently support their children academically.
- How to deal with students who lie about homework.
- How to balance sports, siblings, homework, and everything else.
- How to harness iPods, cell phones, and anything with a screen.

For those of you faced with a problem not addressed earlier in the book, this chapter is for you. Difficult and tricky situations that can challenge even the most seasoned parent will be addressed here.

How To Help Teens Who Resist Adult Support

Living with a teenager is challenging in and of itself; trying to assist a student who may not want help is even more difficult. Teens desire nothing more than independence from their parents. They crave autonomy even though they still want parental feedback and approval. Teens are known for testing parental boundaries and limits. In addition, hormonal changes can wreak havoc on teens' daily moods. One moment an adolescent can seem perfectly secure and happy and the next she can snap over an innocuous comment. Homework and academic expectations add another layer of stress. If this situation sounds familiar, try any one of the following strategies.

The Ball Goes Into Their Court – To parents, teenagers often appear to have all the freedom they could want. After all, they can drive, stay out later in the evening, and have part-time jobs. Frequently, however, their anger comes from the feeling that others have all the power, and they have none. Instead of insisting that your teen accept your homework help, give him a choice. For example, if his biology grade isn't what it should be, ask him if he'd like to work with a study group, stay after school for teacher help, or work with a tutor. Allow him to make the decision of how he will accept help. Getting assistance isn't an option, but the way he obtains it is.

Try This:	Not That:
Give choice of homework assistance. He can accept help after school from a teacher, a student mentor, or professional tutor.	*Giving into one of the two extremes: Sitting next to him to make sure homework is done or expecting him to do everything on his own.*
Give choice of study location such as his room, home office, or basement. Allow a quiet retreat away from parents and siblings. Check in from time to time.	*Planting him at the kitchen table to be certain he is working or allowing him to work unsupervised in his room where he just surfs the net.*
Ask him to create a timeline for project completion.	*Directing him when and how he will start and complete the project.*

Become A Supporter - Be there to offer support and guidance, but resist the urge to correct or provide answers. A good rule of thumb is, "A parent's pen should never touch the paper." Any mark on a student's paper should be his alone. Help him to interpret directions and get started and, if necessary, review the assignment when he's done. Do not criticize wrong answers or he'll be turned off to your help. Teens often don't want to work with their parents because they feel judged, whether their perception is true or not. The assignment just has to meet teacher expectations and reflect the course's guidelines. Striving for perfection can inspire rebellion, especially in adolescents.

Plan Ahead - Arguments over homework often occur at stressful times, especially when a deadline is approaching. Pick one evening every week to preview the upcoming workload. If the week is going to be particularly stressful, determine what extra-curricular activities can be skipped. Teens tend to hunker down and resist support when they're feeling overwhelmed. If this is what's happening in your household, plan a weekly meeting to work out a less hectic schedule. By planning ahead, both you and your student will be more at ease.

Stick To It - Parents often ask me how they can establish routines when their adolescent has his own schedule, friends, and social agenda. The bottom line is that parents of teens should still make the final decisions concerning academics and socializing. Parents can insist that schoolwork comes before socializing or screen time, but allow your teen to choose his homework schedule. For example, if he likes to start after dinner and is able to get it done, then fine. He's more likely to stick with a schedule if he chooses it. Establishing the "work before play" family policy (for all kids, not just your struggling student) is important. It sends the message that school is the number one priority. Enforce this policy consistently, instead of haphazardly, and your teen will adjust in time.

Use Technology – Teenagers these days are extremely tech savvy. Use their interest in everything online or interactive to provide additional support during homework time.

- **Math** – When your teen is resisting your help, identify key websites where he can find support. There are many resources online where students can find additional explanations of topics, problems, or concepts, as well as supplementary practice to reinforce trouble spots.

- **Writing** – There are many software programs out there to help students with all aspects of the writing process, from brainstorming to essay organization. These programs also help students overcome the initial hurdle of "getting started." Check out Inspiration (www.inspiration.com), Co-Writer, and DraftBuilder (www.donjohnston.com).

- **Reading** – If your child struggles with reading, consider utilizing books on tape. Many textbooks have audio versions that allow students to listen to chapters while they follow along in their book, providing both visual and auditory input. These are available through the publishers or online. Be sure that you purchase the full text and not an abridged version. Kurzweil 3000 is a more expensive option, but it allows students to scan in book pages that are "read" to them by the computer. It also includes highlighting and note-taking features that many students find helpful.

Leave It Alone – It can be difficult to decide how much support you should provide your teen as she matures, but it can be the case that the more you "hold her up" the less she learns. Ultimately, providing too much support may cause her to fall even harder down the road. Build a strong foundation to keep her afloat, but know that high school students should function fairly independently. And remember, your teen's actions are not always a reflection of your parenting abilities. At some point, there will be diminishing returns on the work that you put into the situation. Letting your child be a self-sufficient learner may be difficult, but this is a way for her to learn and internalize new skills.

How Working Parents With Limited Time Can Monitor Homework

After a long day at work, one of the last things a working parent wants to come home to is a pile of homework. Kids certainly aren't the only ones who dread it. In fact, a recent LifeCare® poll found that 99 percent of working parents feel some level of stress when trying to help their children with homework—and 49 percent of them rate the stress they feel as "high." Many parents report that their children don't even begin to tackle assignments while they are in after-care or home alone. In addition to dinner, chores, and sports, they now have a full load of homework to complete in a very limited amount of time. More than ever, a working parent must have a few tricks up his or her sleeve to get it all done. Consider these ideas:

Use After-Care To Your Advantage - Talk with the after-care director or teacher responsible for your child. Ask him or her to have your child complete the easiest homework assignment before leaving for the day. Many children either cannot focus or do not want to do homework in after-care, but they are capable of completing a simple task. By the time your child arrives home, at least one piece of work is out of the way.

Plan Time While Home Alone - If you are unable to be at home when your child comes in off the bus, arrange to either call home at a specified time or have your child call you upon arrival. During this conversation, ask your child to share his prioritized homework list, again, ranking work from easy to hard. This way, the simple work is completed early on and you can assist with the more difficult assignments as needed. In addition, encourage your child to check off work he has finished so that you will be able to see quickly and easily what has been accomplished and what is left to do.

Use Weekends Constructively - The weekend provides a wonderful opportunity for working parents to be active supporters of their children's homework. You can create a plan for upcoming projects (pgs. 129 and 130 for project planning forms), study ahead for tests, and preview the coming week. Schedule a Sunday evening check-in to evaluate progress and finalize details for the new week.

Find A Study Buddy - Many elementary classrooms already distribute a list of contact information for classmates. Have your child identify three students he feels comfortable contacting in case he has any questions regarding homework. Keep their contact information in your child's homework area. If your student is older, encourage him to choose several trusted peers or one peer from each class, to call with any questions.

How Divorced Parents Can Provide Consistent Support

Divorce is difficult enough, but throwing homework into the mix can create a new set of issues. These days many custody arrangements are based on a 50/50 split instead of the traditional every other weekend visit. This means that Mom and Dad must work together to ensure that assignments are completed and their children's grades are solid. Successful parents have found that, by setting aside their differences and focusing on the academic tasks at hand, homework need not be a battle. Try one of the tips below and see what works best for you.

Communication Is EVERYTHING – Parents and children benefit from a communication system that ensures both parties are on the same page.

1. For parents who don't like to exchange emails, creating a communication checklist is a great tool. This checklist includes information regarding homework that can be obtained from the child's planner. By recording homework information on a checklist, the receiving parent can easily see what needs to be the focus over the next couple of days. Then, that parent updates the checklist before returning it once again.

Communication  Checklist

Week of _May 3_

Things to bring when switching homes:

- ✓ Backpack
- ✓ Jared's binder
- ✓ Peggy's homework folder
- ✓ Stuffed animals
- ✓ Gym shoes
- ✓ Library books
- ✓ Soccer jersey, cleats, and shin guards

Things to remember this week (from Mom):

- ✓ Peggy has a big social studies test on Thursday. Study flashcards.

Checklist cont.

✓ Chorus practice is a dress rehearsal on Thursday at 5 pm for both.
✓ Jared has library on Friday this week.
✓ School pictures on Friday.

Things to remember this week (from Dad):

✓ Jared needs to practice his oral book report – due on Monday. Can you help him glue the pictures on his poster too?
✓ Jared has a chapter math test on Tuesday.
✓ Peggy's teacher wants a conference. How about Nov. 12 or 13?
✓ She is staying after school on Tuesday for extra help.

2. The checklist can be kept in its own folder titled "Parent Talk." All important papers that need to go back and forth should be placed in this folder as well, including the weekly folders that are common in the elementary grades. This system allows both parents to know where to look for information and where to place new information that is handed out while the child is in their care. This arrangement is helpful because the child does not have to act as a messenger.

3. Adding a monthly calendar to the Parent Talk folder can also be an extremely useful idea. Both parents can easily see and add to the activities scheduled for the coming weeks so that no one will be taken by surprise. After-school activities can be easily set up without having to directly communicate with an ex-spouse.

Some Days Are Better Than Others – Understand that the parent who has custody later in the week may bear the brunt of the homework. Major assignments, tests, and projects are often due at the end of the week. The parent with custody early in the week usually has the lighter load. If you have a choice in the arrangement, the parent who is better able to support academics may want to have custody later in the week to ensure that nothing slips through the cracks and that the student is prepared for the upcoming week.

Understand Limitations – Realize that there are limitations in a person's abilities. The other parent may not be capable or truly know how to assist his child with academic needs. In cases like this, instead of blaming ("My ex can't do anything...I can't trust him to help the kids with homework"), let go of what you can't control. Use weekends or nights with minimal homework to get ahead. It simply is what it is and negativity toward the other parent will not improve the academic situation.

Show Up Together (or Apart) – It's very helpful for both parents to attend Back to School Night, parent conferences, and other school meetings. If this is not feasible because of your current relationship, schedule two conferences or attend the alternate day of informational sessions. By understanding the school's expectations up front, later disagreements can be avoided.

Present A Unified Front – Adhere to the same schedules, rewards, and consequences as much as possible. Sit down with your ex-spouse, have a phone conversation, or begin an email correspondence about how to discipline consistently. If this hasn't been done in the past, consider beginning at the start of a week, month, or new grading period. Here are some questions to consider:

What daily routines will be in place?

What schedule will be adhered to at each home?

What are the academic expectations?

Once the answers to these questions have been agreed upon, then begin discussing rewards, consequences and what is and is not acceptable.

When both parents are generally in agreement, children are less able to manipulate situations to their benefit. They may certainly try with the usual "But that's how Mom does it," or "Dad lets me do that," but parental consistency will limit these attempts.

How To Deal With Students Who Lie About Homework

"I did that homework in class."
"It's not due until the end of the month – really!"
"I turned it in – I swear."

Students who lie about homework aren't inherently bad; they are usually looking for a way out of an uncomfortable situation. Lying is an instantaneous way to reduce the outside pressure of schoolwork (although the long-term effects are just as stressful). In most cases, students are simply trying to dodge the truth—that the work is too hard, they don't understand it, or that they don't know how to begin. The pattern can easily become habitual, especially as the lies begin to build and accumulate.

Determine WHY The Lies Occur - The first step to dealing with lying is to uncover why your child feels the need to be untruthful. Acknowledge his reasons, be understanding, but don't condone the behavior. For example, if your child routinely lies about completing his math homework, it could be due to the fact that he just doesn't understand the math concepts he is working on in class. Talk to the teacher and ask for the teacher's impression of your child's mastery of the material. If possible, try to help your child with the work, but remember—be patient! If you erupt in anger, it will encourage your child to continue lying to avoid your reactions.

Praise The Truth - Praise your child when he's upfront about overdue work or a bad grade. Once he's filled you in on what has really been going on, work out a solution to the problem by arranging for extra help. When he realizes that you are on his side, he'll come to you more regularly when experiencing difficulty.

Double The Penalty - There should be no surprises when it comes to consequences. Because honest communication is so important, penalties should increase if a child lies about what he did or did not do. Consequences should be stated very clearly before the behavior occurs. Better yet, they should be written down and posted. Let's examine some very common scenarios.

Peggy - Hiding the Truth

After Peggy completed her math homework, her father, John notices three mistakes. When he asks her to make corrections, she refuses. He calmly says, "The rule in this house is that cell phone access is only allowed after your homework is done and corrected. You have 30 minutes to correct these problems." A half hour later, Peggy tells John that she has completed the corrections. Upon review, he realizes that she didn't even attempt the work. John informs Peggy that she loses the use of her cell phone that night and the next day. He doubled the penalty for lying.

Richard - Trying to Cover His Tracks

Richard has been reminded three times to bring his social studies book home. His mom even puts a sticky note in his planner as a visual reminder and tells him that if the book doesn't come home, he can't go to the school play. The next day, Richard forgets again. Because he's dying to go to the play, he lies and says it's in his book bag. Upon discovering the truth, he isn't allowed to attend the play and is restricted from the following evening's activity.

Cynthia - Preoccupied with Friends

It is a family policy in the Dunn household that the children complete two of their easiest homework assignments before their parents return home from work at 5:30 pm. One evening, Cynthia is so busy chatting on the phone with a friend that she neglects to even begin her work. Her mother asks why she didn't start the assignments and Cynthia fudges the truth. She contends this isn't a big deal because the teachers don't grade the work; therefore, she really doesn't have to do it. Her mother restricts her from TV for two evenings, one for not doing the work and the second for not accepting responsibility for her act of omission. Homework is homework, whether it's graded or not.

Recognize Other Warning Signs - Be mindful of the stresses that your child is facing in and out of school. Remember that students often react to social, substance abuse, and emotional issues by shutting down on their schoolwork. If you suspect that lying is a coping mechanism for a larger issue, be sure to consult a mental health professional.

Balancing Sports, Siblings, Homework, Etc. When EVERYTHING Feels Overwhelming

This is the parenting question of the decade and I often wonder if our own parents ever felt this way years ago when they were raising us. I'm sure they did to an extent, but now life seems so much more hurried, stressful, and complicated. Try the following solutions to make life a little simpler.

Reassess The After-School Schedule - In a recent KidsHealth survey, almost 90 percent of students said they felt stressed. That's an alarming statistic. However, I'm sure we can all agree that each child is different – some thrive on hectic schedules, whereas others crave downtime. Listening to our kids is the only way we'll know how they feel. Take time to ask your child if his load is too stressful, or just right.

The flip side of this equation is your personal situation. Perhaps more than children, parents feel overextended and exhausted. Managing kids, a job, transportation to sports, and of course, homework, is enough to put even the most organized and efficient parent through the wringer. If this feels too familiar, consider reexamining your children's schedules. Can one activity go by the wayside? Is there a sport or lesson that your child doesn't truly enjoy, but you insisted upon so that he doesn't miss out on an opportunity? These are the activities you might want to reconsider.

Recently, a neighbor of mine with three children realized that she just could not function with the amount of driving and carpooling she was doing after school. Homework was taking a back seat to sports, so she had her kids each choose just one activity they wanted to participate in for the season. She said this simple decision decreased household stress remarkably.

Create A Predictable Schedule – Although each child in your household is likely to have a different schedule, it helps to make a family policy that homework must at least be started before leaving for an after-school activity.

Use A White Board - It's easy to keep track of assignments with a white board. Hang a large white board near an area that will be used for homework. When your children return from school each day, insist that they write their assignments on the white board. Be sure they are prioritized (1, 2, 3) and that the child crosses off each task as it's completed. By using this tool, you or any other adult in the home will know of the assignments each child has for the day, what has been completed, and what is still left to do. When the homework assignment list is visible, unfinished work is less likely to slip through the cracks. This is a great solution for busy households.

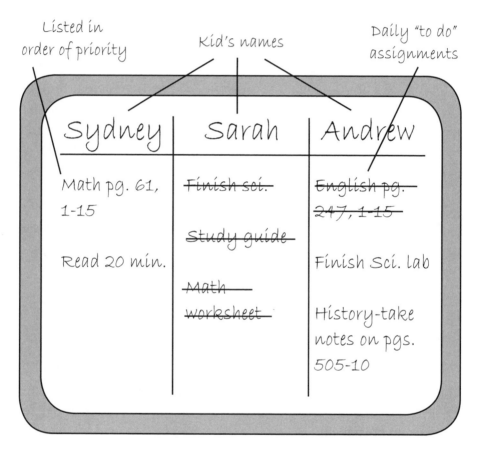

Use Spiral-Bound Cards – Oxford makes spiral-bound index cards in neon and white which can be purchased at www.shoplet.com. As an alternative to the white board, provide each child with a set to record daily homework. Each day's assignments are written on a separate card they can refer to while completing homework. The notecards can be stored on hooks designated for each child.

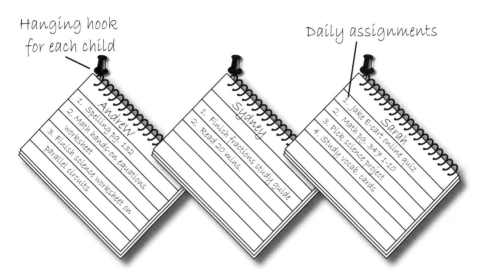

Hanging hook for each child

Daily assignments

Andrew
1. Spelling pg. 132
2. Math hands-on equations worksheet
3. Finish science worksheet on parallel circuits

Sydney
1. Finish fractions study guide
2. Read 20 mins.

Sarah
1. Jake E-cart online quiz
2. Math pg. 347 1-10
3. Pick science project
4. Study vocab. cards

Conduct An Audit – Busy parents know that it's difficult to check every assignment each child has night after night. The Internal Revenue Service keeps taxpayers in line with random audits. You can do the same in your home.

The four kids in the Murray family know that homework must be done by 8 pm. That's always been the household rule. Mr. and Mrs. Murray have a hard enough time managing full-time jobs and four kids' busy schedules in addition to homework. They cannot religiously check each child's homework every night, so they use the audit method. On any given night, Mom or Dad can ask to see the homework. If it's not done, that child can't leave the house after school the following day to see friends, nor can he or she watch TV.

One evening, Dad asked to see Justine's homework. She said it was done, but amazingly, couldn't locate it. Dad revisits the issue in 10 minutes. Justine confesses to not completing it. Now she misses out on her free time the following evening AND the night afterwards. She will have to adhere to the consequence for not having her work done and for lying about it.

Take A One-Hour Time Out – A one-hour time out is meant to be time away from anything that flashes, beeps, or has a screen. Choose 60 minutes every weekday (the hour immediately following dinner works well) and make that a mandatory quiet time. In our fast paced world, we're bombarded by loud noises which can cause over-stimulation, agitation, and anxiety. During this time, there are no iPods, televisions, video games, computers, or phones. Instead, consider activities such as reading independently or together, doing a puzzle or playing cards. You may find that simply leaving craft supplies out encourages creativity. A one-hour time out also forces kids who would usually be glued to electronics to go outside to play or get together with neighborhood friends.

How To Corral The Power Of iPods, Cell Phones, And Anything Else With A Screen

Technology has transformed our world, but for our kids, life without gadgets would be unimaginable. They expect to have access to these devices 24/7, but their expectations and reality are very different. Technology can be an asset to learning. It can also be a significant detractor unless parents establish clear policies and consequences.

About a month ago, I was speaking to a group of parents at a local school. One mother raised her hand and said that she just couldn't get her daughter to stop texting during homework. I asked her if she would consider taking away the phone. She looked at me, frowned, and said, "I can't possibly do that. She'd go nuts. All the kids text; that's just how it is." She was correct – most kids do text, but this mom had not set boundaries for her daughter. If the overuse of technology is affecting your child's schoolwork, you must set limits. This starts with an electronics-free routine.

- When your child returns from school, allow screen access for a short period of time – about a half hour. Then it goes off.

- It's perfectly acceptable to take the phone, iPod, or other device away from your child if he is sneaking access.

- Agree on a time that you will return their electronics. In my house, it is 7:30 pm, which is about one hour after dinner, following quiet time.

Numerous Parents Ask –

What if he needs his phone to take to sports' practices or after-school clubs?

Let him take it. You can't control everything. The main idea is to have a technology-free homework period.

What if he needs the computer for research?

This is a good question that I hear over and over. The answer is allow him to print out information needed for the writing portion of the assignment. That way, he'll have the information, but won't have continuous and distracting access to the internet.

What if he needs to type his homework?

Another valid question. If your teen has a desk and computer in his room, it should have Word and other Office Suite programs only. By having the computer hooked up to the internet, you may be inviting a whole host of other problems.

What should I do if I see him online or texting when he should be doing homework?

After you've established a "no screen time" policy and window of time that this rule is in place, you must enforce it. Let's say your policy is in effect from 5:30 pm to 6:30 pm. If he breaks the rule, penalize him an hour and restrict his use until 7:30 pm.

She says she focuses better when multitasking. Could this be true?

No. In fact, studies show that when kids continually multitask, they lose the ability to focus on one thing at a time. Picture your daughter with earphones in while listening to her iPod, texting furiously, and checking her Facebook page all at the same time. This is common, but not productive. The problem is that when kids try to concentrate on just one task, such as reading or studying, they're less able to sustain attention because they are so accustomed to stimulation from multiple sources. Even though you can discourage this type of behavior, you cannot stop it. You can, however, eliminate it during homework time.

She says she can't focus without music. Should I allow her to listen?

There may be something to her claims. Studies show that the majority of kids do attend better with background music, but the music should be instrumental. A happy medium between her lyrical music and no music at all, is an iPod filled with songs that you've downloaded. Lower-end iPods are fairly inexpensive. Keep a "homework iPod" on hand for all of your kids to use.

Chapter 12

Putting It All Together

In this chapter you will learn to:

- Prioritize your child's needs even if he has the traits of many profiles.

- Create your own personal Parent Action Plan.

- Reach out for help if your child is resistant.

- Find the right tutor based on experience, methodology, and personality.

- Praise small improvements.

- Honor the unique parent/child bond you have with your child.

At this point in the book you should feel equipped to transform tense homework struggles into a predictable, productive experience. But you may also be wondering how exactly to get started if your child fits multiple homework problem profiles.

What If My Child Fits Into All Six Profiles?

One question that I am asked time and again is, "What if my child fits into more than one of these categories?" It's not at all uncommon for students to have traits of many profiles and to fit into multiple categories. The key here is to focus on your child's most pressing issue. For example, if his biggest issue is inattention, start there. If he's doing poorly across the board, but you think his issues are rooted in disorganization, begin with the strategies in Chapter 4.

The Problem

Christian's Not-So-Unusual Story

Christian Carter is the kind of kid teachers enjoy having in class. He takes direction well, gets along with his classmates, and is a solid B student. If only homework was so simple! Just getting Christian to start his daily work is a struggle, not to mention those long-term reports. His parents are fed up with his last minute ways and realize they need to take control of the after-school hours.

Christian has characteristics of many profiles in this book, but Mr. and Mrs. Carter feel that procrastination is by far his biggest obstacle. They also realize that they must tread lightly. Christian will not be receptive to sweeping changes as a budding teen at 12 years old. After dinner one evening, they discuss their concerns with him and together, the family agrees on changes.

Meredith and Tom Carter are realistic parents. They dreamed of instant success, but they soon realized that their wishful thinking was just that. Because they had been through some of these issues with their older daughter, they knew the key was to target the behaviors that were impacting Christian the most. They created a Parent Action Plan to help guide them initially. You can use the same plan to make positive changes in your home.

Create A Parent Action Plan

A Parent Action Plan is your own personal "how to" guide to ease homework stress. By taking time to write down just a few goals, you'll be further committed and more likely to stay the course. To create a plan, you should:

1. Identify one or two problems that are causing the most distress.

2. Craft specific goals related to these issues.

3. Write down one to three strategies you can realistically implement to achieve this goal. Ask yourself, "Can I honestly do this for the rest of the school year?"

4. Implement these strategies.

5. Assess progress after one week and then again after 21 days.

6. Once you consistently see change, pull back slightly so that you are less involved and your child has ownership over the strategy.

The issue that was causing the most stress in the Carter household was Christian's chronic procrastination. Meredith and Tom decided that beginning homework earlier in the day was crucial for their son and they set up two simple steps to help him achieve it.

Goal	Steps
Start homework earlier in the day.	1. Christian will fill out a Time Management Chart each Sunday evening, recording daily start times. Parents will initial and post on the refrigerator. 2. Christian will have access to his phone upon homework completion.

After the first week of everyone adhering to this goal, Meredith and Tom reflected back with pride. By simply taking possession of the cell phone after school, there were fewer arguments. Christian had to earn it by completing his homework and making any corrections they requested. In addition, he started to see the value of daily planning. The Time Management Chart helped him to realize that competitive hockey took up a lot of his after-school hours. Having a set homework start time before practice allowed Christian to feel less stressed in the evening.

In a month's time, the Carters fell into a predictable routine; however, there were two occasions when Christian panicked the night before projects were due. He underestimated the length of time it would take him to produce a research paper and prepare an oral presentation. After staying up until 1 am, he finally finished the work. The Carters added another goal for long-term planning because this issue had surfaced regularly over the last few years. Christian was less than excited, but he agreed when his parents assured him there would be no more badgering; the ball was in his court.

Goal	Steps
Plan projects in advance.	1. On Sunday evenings, Christian will identify any long-term projects and complete a Project Planning Guide form.

2. Christian will post the form on the refrigerator door.

3. Parents may not nag about upcoming dates. |

Meredith and Tom reviewed the progress Christian had made. Just the other day, Christian asked his mom if she could purchase poster board for him. Although this seemed like a minor request, it was huge – he needed it for a project that wasn't due for another week. Not only did Meredith commend her son at that moment, but she made a point to praise him during the family dinner that evening.

After about a month, Christian was able to begin and complete his homework early in the day (before dinner) without prompting. The Time Management Chart had served its purpose and was no longer necessary on a weekly basis. Christian and his parents agreed to revisit it if he started slipping back into his old habits. The one intervention they weren't ready to relinquish was planning long-term assignments in advance. They decided to continue using the Project Planning Guide each Sunday for another month. If at that time, Christian was on top of his work, they would move to an every-other-week meeting. By providing Christian with solutions to his struggles, supporting his needs, and then slowly decreasing their involvement, they helped make lasting changes.

Now It's Your Turn!

Take five minutes to write an action plan that addresses your child's most pressing issue. Put your long-term vision of stress-free homework into a short-term action plan. To get you started, I've included the following blank Parent Action form. Begin documenting one or two goals and the steps you'll follow.

Although you may be tempted to skip this step, close this book, and roll up your sleeves to get started, I urge you to take the time to put your thoughts onto paper. You'll be more likely to remember and successfully implement strategies if you commit them to writing.

Parent Action Plan

Goal	Steps
	1.
	2.
	3.

Remember – Your child's habits have evolved over time, so it will take time and effort to get results. When parents fail to see positive outcomes, it's usually because they have fallen into one of four traps.

1. They bite off more than they can chew. Homework problems are best solved by simple modifications, not unsustainable major overhauls. Choose one problem area and start there with just a few interventions. Focus on a couple of ideas that you are sure to stick with for the remainder of the school year.

2. They don't involve the student in making decisions. Include your children in discussions so that they feel a part of the household and the decision-making process. It's less likely that they will rebel if they feel some ownership over the changes that will be taking place.

3. They give up when resistance is encountered. Kids are creatures of habit, just like adults. Most like it their way, or no way. Expect them to push back in the beginning; that's normal. Don't let your child's behavior deter you. Stick with the interventions you have in place for three weeks.

4. They experience success, so they stop using the strategies. When you see that what you're doing is working, keep on doing it. For example, if your teen has become more organized because you taught her a binder system and check in with her regularly, don't expect her to sustain neatness without you. Stick with bi-weekly meetings until she demonstrates that she can stay organized from one check-in to the next. Only then, move your meetings to every other week.

What If My Child Won't Let Me Help Him?

Sometimes, parents aren't the best teachers for their child because of the many emotional layers that naturally define this relationship. You may find that you can help with the basics such as routines and rewards and consequences. When it comes to study skills, reading strategies, and organization systems, an objective third party can be the key to turning your child around.

In my tutoring practice, I frequently hear parents say, "He won't listen to me, but he'll listen to his tutor." A tutor does not have an emotional history with the child like a parent, and she, therefore, may be able to break through to even the most challenging student. Even if your child is hesitant about outside help, go ahead and try it anyway. After the first session or two, he will likely let down his guard when he sees that learning doesn't have to be so difficult. If possible, enlist support early on. A bad report card grade can be the impetus for seeking assistance, but by then, you're child may already feel defeated.

The Carters found that a tutor made an incredible difference in Christian's approach to studying. Meredith and Tom were able to assist with their son's issues involving procrastination and planning, but recognized he was not at all open to learning better study strategies and test-taking techniques from them. Their observations were accurate. Most of the time, kids take direction better from an outsider rather than their parents, especially as they get older. In your family, you may find that detaching yourself from homework, the source of conflict, is actually therapeutic for the parent/child relationship. I know I have!

Due to my regular evening speaking commitments, I've found it helpful to hire a tutor to assist both of my children with their homework on a weekly basis. The night before the boys' new tutor began, I mentioned to my older son that we should consider creating a monthly calendar, since this quarter he would be having multiple projects. His response was "Mom, I don't need to do that this year. I can remember it all in my head." I didn't press the issue, but did mention it to his tutor, Gayle. The next evening, she came for an initial session. Afterward, I asked them how it went. My son said, "Great, Mom! We got so much done. We even put all my projects on this cool calendar!" I bit my tongue. Wait a second – wasn't that the same suggestion I made to him just a night before? Of course it was, but he was willing to follow-through because the idea came from someone else.

Finding The Right Fit

At my company, my staff and I spend a great deal of time speaking with parents about their children's educational needs and matching them with the right tutor. We take into account experience, subject area specialty, and most importantly, personality. If you decide that a private tutor could be an asset to your child, make sure the person you choose has:

1. The right background – Be sure her experience is in line with your needs. Elementary students need a tutor who has classroom teaching experience. Although teaching certification isn't imperative, it is helpful. Older students needing assistance in math or science must have a subject specialist, someone who understands the curriculum and is a content area expert.

2. The right methodology – The way the material is taught is vital. For students with weak organization or study skills, the tutor cannot merely help with homework. This is a waste of time. The instructor must have experience in three areas – a binder system, daily prioritization and long-term planning, and study skills. These skills cannot be taught in isolation either. The skill set has to be applied to the student's daily homework so that she can see the real life benefit.

3. The right personality – Some students are resistant to help, therefore, making sure that the tutor you select has the right personality will make all the difference. We often ask parents, "What type of person will your child respond to?" or "Describe the type of teacher she's really enjoyed in the past." When a student forms a positive relationship with the tutor, he's much more willing to put forth effort.

Praise Small Improvements

The last step in knowing you're on the right track is to notice and praise small changes. Christian still needed a reminder to start his homework, but one was certainly better than the four or five reminders he used to require. He was making progress managing procrastination.

Look for small improvements in your child, too. Far too often, we want quick fixes and immediate gratification, but real and lasting change takes time. I've worked with many students who required a full school year of support before they began internalizing study skills.

Even at that point, they still needed monitoring. Try to view your child as if you haven't seen him in six months. Is he maturing, working more independently, or remembering his materials more than before? If so, you're making progress.

You may see that your child takes two steps forward, but then one step back. This is perfectly normal; don't give up when the step back occurs. It may last for just an hour, a day, or even a week, but stay the course. Your child will turn the corner.

When you're frustrated working with your child, please remember a line of practical advice from well-known psychiatrist, Dr. Russell Barkley -- "Don't sacrifice your parent/child relationship on the altar of academic performance." His message reinforces that the unique bond you have with your child is far more important than any one homework assignment.

It's my hope that you found this guide beneficial and learned many practical strategies and tools to take the stress out of homework and, more importantly, to maintain that special relationship with your child.

I wish you the very best on your road to - Homework Made Simple!

Resources

Books

Borba, M. *The Big Book of Parenting Solutions: 101 Answers to Your Everyday Challenges and Wildest Worries.* Jossey-Bass, 2009. Offers advice for the wide array of behavioral challenges parents face with their children.

Brooks, R. and S. Goldstein. *Raising Resilient Children: Fostering Strength, Hope, and Optimism in Your Child.* McGraw-Hill, 2002. Explains how parents can best cultivate resiliency in their child by fostering a nurturing environment in the home.

Carlson, B. and W. Doherty. *Putting Family First: Successful Strategies for Reclaiming Life in a Hurry-up World.* Holt Paperbacks, 2002. As founders of a family advocacy organization, these authors speak on the importance of making family a priority once again.

Cohen, C. *Raise Your Child's Social IQ: Stepping Stones to People Skills for Kids.* Advantage Books, 2000. Provides parents with a structural framework to work with their children on social skills and awareness.

Cooper, H. *The Battle Over Homework: Common Ground for Administrators, Teachers, and Parents.* Corwin Press, 2006. This is a good guide for educators to hold constructive discussions with families about homework.

Dawson, P. and R. Guare. *Smart but Scattered: The Revolutionary "Executive Skills" Approach to Helping Kids Reach Their Potential.* The Guilford Press, 2009. Easy to follow steps to discover your child's strengths and weaknesses and techniques to improve upon them.

Dietzel, L. and J. Cooper-Kahn. *Late, Lost, and Unprepared: A Parents' Guide to Helping Children with Executive Functioning.* Woodbine House, 2008. Provides parents with suggestions to help their child build strong executive functioning skills.

Dweck, C. *Mindset: The New Psychology of Success.* Ballantine Books, 2007. An inspirational book that challenges our idea of a fixed mindset and proposes new ideas for increasing motivation.

Fox, J. *Get Organized without Losing It.* Free Spirit Publishing, 2006. This is a fun and practical guide for kids to reduce stress and learn organizational skills. It is full of tips, strategies, and examples.

Frender, G. *Learning to Learn: Strengthening Study Skills and Brain Power.* Incentive Publications, 2004. This book is filled with hints and ideas for students to learn more effectively and provides hands-on materials for important study skills.

Goldberg, D. and J. Zweibel. *The Organized Student: Teaching Children the Skills for Success in School and Beyond.* Fireside, 2005. This book lays out step-by-step strategies for getting organized.

Goldstein, S. and S. Zentall. *Seven Steps to Homework Success-A Family Guide for Solving Common Homework Problems.* Specialty Press, 1998. Contains questionnaires to determine sources of homework difficulties and provides tips to address them.

Weiss, S. and J. Heininger. *From Chaos to Calm: Effective Parenting for Challenging Children with ADHD and Other Behavior Problems.* Perigee Trade, 2001. Using the point of view of a parent, therapist, and child, this book compiles a helpful guide for those working with children with ADHD and other behavioral issues.

Lavoie, R. *The Motivation Breakthrough: 6 Secrets to Turning on the Tuned-out Child.* Touchstone, 2008. This book emphasizes motivational factors for children and offers strategies to encourage your child's success.

Levine, M. *The Myth of Laziness.* Simon & Schuster, 2003. Offers explanations for unproductive students and provides insight for their success in school.

Moss, S., L. Schwartz, and M. Wertz. *Where's My Stuff?: The Ultimate Teen Organizing Guide.* Orange Avenue Publishing, 2007. Filled with great organizational strategies for school and home.

Parker, H. *Put Yourself in Their Shoes: Understanding Teenagers with Attention Deficit Disorder.* Specialty Press, 1999. Although written primarily for parents, this book helps anyone understand what it is like to live with ADD.

Phelen, T. *1-2-3 Magic: Effective Discipline for Children 2-12.* Child Management, 1995. Phelen gives straightforward methods for discipline with an emphasis on reacting with little emotion to your child's outbursts.

Power, T. *Homework Success for Children with ADHD. A Family-School Intervention Program.* The Guilford Press, 2001. Details effective ways to implement interventions in order to build healthy home-school relationships and foster your child's self-esteem.

Quinn, P. *Attention, Girls! : A Guide to Learn All about Your ADHD.* Magination Press, 2009. Helps girls discover the many faces of ADHD and learn ways to handle almost any problem they are having.

Romain, T. *How to Do Homework without Throwing Up.* Free Spirit Publishing, 1997. A fun approach to addressing homework skills; directed at young readers.

Rotz, R. and S. Wright. *Fidget to Focus: Outwit Your Boredom: Sensory Strategies for Living with ADD.* iUniverse, Inc., 2005. A practical guide to living with and managing ADD successfully.

Stern, J. and U. Ben-Ami. *Many Ways to Learn: Young People's Guide to Learning Disabilities, Revised.* Magination Press, 2010. Challenges children to think about their strengths as well as their weaknesses.

Vatterott, C. *Rethinking Homework: Best Practices That Support Diverse Needs.* ASCD, 2009. This book focuses on the importance of homework quality versus quantity and discusses the role of homework in modern day education.

Weinfeld, R., S. Jeweler, L. Barnes-Robinson, and B. Shevitz. *Smart Kids with Learning Difficulties: Overcoming Obstacles and Realizing Potential.* Prufrock Press, 2006. Provides useful advice for bright kids to overcome learning challenges.

Zeigler Dendy, C. *Teaching Teens with ADD and ADHD—A Quick Reference Guide for Teachers and Parents.* Woodbine House, 2000. A great handbook for teachers and parent alike. It summarizes important issues related to ADHD and success in school.

Products

BINDERS: www.caseit.com - *The best binders on the market. Check out the S-815 and S-915 binders with built-in accordion folders.*

EXERCISE BALL CHAIR: www.sitincomfort.com - *An alternative to the traditional chair to sit in during homework; great for kids who tend to fidget.*

HIGHLIGHTING TAPE, EZC READER AND MYSTERY MOTIVATOR: *www.reallygoodstuff.com - Highlighter tape can be used in texts when markers cannot be used. The EZC reader helps guide a reader's eye and Mystery Motivators provide exciting rewards.*

GRAPHIC ORGANIZERS: www.graphicorganizers.com - *Visual webs and outlines to help students organize information.*

LAP DESK: www.roomitup.com - *A lap pad desk with a flat writing surface as another alternative to sitting at a desk.*

LOCKER SUPPLIES: www.schoolpak.com, www.raymondgeddes. com, and www.locker-works.com - *School lockers look cool and stay organized at the same time.*

MAGNETIC WEEKLY CALENDAR: www.organizedstudent.com - *This calendar attaches to the refrigerator and can be used to keep track of all family members' activities in one central location.*

MOM AGENDA WEEKLY CALENDAR: *www.momagenda.com – Unique weekly planner with enough space to fit the schedules of Mom and up to four children each day.*

MARK-MY-TIME: www.mark-my-time.com - *A bookmark-style timer for timing independent reading.*

MULTIPLICATION QUIZ CUBE: www.carsondellosa.com - *An inflatable ball labeled with math facts. A fun way to practice multiplication instead of using flash cards.*

PRIZE REINFORCERS: www.smilemakers.com - *Offers a wide array of low-cost reinforcers such as stickers and toys that can be used for home reward systems.*

RECORDABLE PEN: www.livescribe.com and www.amazon.com - *Voice recordable pen for students who resist writing down their assignments.*

SPELL CHECKER: www.franklin.com - *The Franklin Spelling Ace with Thesaurus is a handheld device that provides phonetic spell correction for over 100,000 words.*

SPINNERS: www.reallygoodstuff.com - *The Write Again® Dry Erase Open Ended Spinner Kit is a great way to practice a skill or reward your child, with just a spin of the dial.*

THE STUDY ZONE: www.strategiceducationalsolutions.com - *A portable homework and study station.*

TANGLE JR.: www.tanglecreations.com - *Twistable fidget toy to help with focus.*

TIME TIMER: www.timetimer.com - *This timer ensures that time awareness is easy to understand and monitor by depicting the passage of time visually.*

TRAFFIC LIGHT TIMER: www.callowayhouse.com - *Stoplight timer for younger students who benefit from both auditory and visual reminders of elapsed time.*

TYPING SOFTWARE: www.amazon.com - *"Typing Quick and Easy" and "Type to Learn" are engaging video game format programs that make learning to keyboard a cinch.*

WATCHMINDER: www.watchminder.com - *Watch with silent reminder to help students stay on task.*

WEIGHTED LAP PADS: www.flaghouse.com - *Soft weighted pad that can be laid across a student's lap while completing homework. Can help with attention and focus.*

WRITING SOFTWARE: www.inspiration.com and www.donjohnston.com - *Excellent programs to assist students who need to get over the hurdle of planning and organizing their thoughts.*

Websites

Addvance.com - *A website for information on ADHD. Particularly helpful for parents of girls with the disorder.*

Chadd.org - *A site full of helpful information that provides education, advocacy, and support for those living with ADHD.*

Childdevelopmentinfo.com - *Provides information and resources for parents dealing with different stages of their child's development.*

Ed.gov/parents - *Department of Education website filled with resources for parents on a variety of topics including homework help, special needs, college information, and academic success.*

Familyeducation.com - *Great website filled with information and activities for families and children.*

Greatschools.com - *National non-profit whose mission is "to inspire and guide parents to become effective champions of their children's education at home and in their communities."*

Homeworkmadesimple.com - *Host of articles and resources for parents of children struggling with homework.*

Ldonline.org - *A leading website on learning disabilities and ADHD full of resources for educators, parents, and kids including articles, advice, and support.*

Math-and-reading-help-for-kids.org - *Articles on homework help written by educational professionals.*

Readingrockets.com - *Excellent website for young readers and those who struggle with reading.*

Studygs.net - *Outstanding resource filled with tips and strategies for studying, time management, problem solving, and other skills for successful learning.*